LESSONS IN PSYCHOANALYSIS

LESSONS IN PSYCHOANALYSIS
Psychopathology and Clinical Psychoanalysis for Trainee Analysts

Franco De Masi

PHOENIX
PUBLISHING HOUSE
firing the mind

First published in 2023 by
Phoenix Publishing House Ltd
62 Bucknell Road
Bicester
Oxfordshire OX26 2DS

Copyright © 2023 by Franco De Masi

The right of Franco De Masi to be identified as the author of this work has been asserted in accordance with §§ 77 and 78 of the Copyright Design and Patents Act 1988.

All rights reserved. No part of this publication may be reproduced, stored in a retrieval system, or transmitted, in any form or by any means, electronic, mechanical, photocopying, recording, or otherwise, without the prior written permission of the publisher.

British Library Cataloguing in Publication Data

A C.I.P. for this book is available from the British Library

ISBN-13: 978-1-912691-88-3

Typeset by Medlar Publishing Solutions Pvt Ltd, India

www.firingthemind.com

Contents

About the author   vii
Author's note   viii
Introduction   ix

Chapter 1: On the specific nature of psychoanalysis   1

Chapter 2: Making a diagnosis in psychoanalysis   5

Chapter 3: The significance of history   11

Chapter 4: Psychoanalytic theories   17

Chapter 5: The unconscious and emotional reality   25

Chapter 6: Non-validation of emotional experience   31

Chapter 7: Transference and the analytic relationship   37

Chapter 8: Impasse   43

Chapter 9: Countertransference	47
Chapter 10: Regression	57
Chapter 11: Anxiety	65
Chapter 12: Phobia and panic	75
Chapter 13: Trauma	85
Chapter 14: Identity and psychopathology	97
Chapter 15: Melancholic depression	109
Chapter 16: Non-melancholic depression	121
Chapter 17: Narcissism	131
Chapter 18: Psychic withdrawal	141
Chapter 19: Final considerations	149
References	155
Index	163

About the author

Franco De Masi is a training analyst of the Italian Psychoanalytical Society and former President of the Centro Milanese di Psicoanalisi and Secretary of the Training Institute of Milan. He is a medical doctor and a psychiatrist who has worked for many years in psychiatric hospitals. For the last forty years, he has worked as a full-time psychoanalyst in Milan. He has published several papers in *The International Journal of Psychoanalysis*, the *Rivista Italiana di Psicoanalisi*, and other psychoanalytic journals. His main interests are the theoretical and technical psychoanalytical issues related to severely ill or psychotic patients. He is the author and editor of numerous books, including *A Psychoanalytic Approach to Treating Psychosis: Genesis, Psychopathology and Case Study* (Routledge, 2020).

Author's note

For ease of reading, when non-specific situations are being referred to, "he" is used throughout but the points raised are applicable to all.

Introduction

Inspiration for this book has been drawn from a series of my lessons with pupils over a number of years at the Milanese Section of the National Institute of Training of the Italian Psychoanalytical Society. Several students recorded and transcribed the lessons, which they then passed on to the Training Secretary, who made them available to whoever requested a copy. It was then suggested by some colleagues that I publish these, since trainee analysts could find them useful, as could those analysts who continue to raise questions about the specific nature of the psychoanalytic discipline. I have chosen, I believe, the most important lessons and added a few new chapters that may enrich parts strictly related to psychopathology and psychoanalytic clinical work.

The first chapters are an overview of the scientific status of psychoanalysis, its main theories and models, and the way in which the unconscious registers emotional reality. Topics that are closer to clinical work then follow, such as the issue of diagnosis in psychoanalysis and the importance of the patient's clinical history. Following that, I have written on the transference and the analytic relationship, two distinct entities of cardinal importance in clinical work, in my view, and in the two chapters that follow, I look at the analytic impasse and a moderate use of the countertransference. Regression, anxiety, phobia, and panic are then considered, which, together with trauma, have been widely studied throughout the development of psychoanalytic thought. One entire chapter is then dedicated to depersonalisation in various syndromes, followed by other chapters on melancholic and non-melancholic depression, given the considerable difference in their dynamics. Narcissism, with its related problems, and then the psychic withdrawal are examined in the final chapters, which are dedicated to clinical work. In the last chapter, I conclude with a short discussion on several aspects related to analytic therapy.

In some parts of the book, the topic in question is preceded by a description of how ideas evolved and then went on to form a concept. Analytic concepts are not linear but fashioned from numerous stratifications that form over time. To fully understand an analytic conceptualisation, we cannot ignore its trajectory or any points along the way. From its birth, any analytic concept is endowed with flexibility that, up to a point, allows new contributions to be assimilated without its specific meaning being lost in the process.

In addition, when it seems useful, I refer to some data from neuroscientific research. I believe it is helpful to report *in parallel* what neuroscience has to tell us about those phenomena that are also studied by psychoanalysts, without seeking, however, to forcibly favour hybridisation, the result of which could be confusing or misleading.

This book also aims to contribute to broadening and examining in-depth psychoanalytic clinical work. Contrary to current practice, which centres on the analyst's mind at work, my belief, as shall be clearer after reading the chapter on countertransference, is that the analyst's fantasies and imagination cannot be placed in the foreground in analytic work but must be connected to and justified by early childhood experiences of the patient, whose specific history and psychopathology need to be important focal points.

Frequently, the word psychopathology is considered as pathologising. If, however, we leave preconceived judgement to one side, we can see that the clinical approach is founded upon psychopathology; it is the basic component which permeates and structures the analytic process and marks moments of impasse as well as moments of transformation. More precisely, we may say that there is constant dialectic tension between psychopathology and the tool kit the analyst uses to understand and to bring about change.

In this book, the study of psychopathology is *the* element that grounds the clinical approach. What I wish to highlight is the importance that psychopathology and psychoanalytic clinical work have in making psychoanalysis one unitary body. And because of this unitary structure, psychoanalysis can allow various models and theories to coexist and be continually compared, at times resulting in their dialogue but at others in their conflict.

Despite it sometimes being underlined, it is untrue that when analysts meet the patient, they all fail to consider a diagnosis: being close to the patient is a prerequisite, but this should not take away from the therapeutic task. Even when analysts feel close to the patient from the very beginning, they still need to infer the pathogenic forces that operate in the analysand and cause his suffering. If these forces are not pinpointed and treated, there can be no therapy.

It is extremely important to reflect on the ways in which an analyst relates with his patient. Schematically speaking, we may say that there are two common tendencies in contemporary psychoanalytic clinical work: the first maintains that therapy should be specific for each patient; the second, however, sees general principles that are valid with all patients. The former sees each patient as a specific case that requires a selective approach based on the patient's story and the reasons behind his suffering. It appears to me, however, that currently the idea of homogeneity is prevalent; according to this, the psyche is structured by a global organising principle, this view bringing with it the idea that the analyst can analyse the patient without taking into account his specific pathological condition. Engaging, however, with the immense diversity in clinical pictures that we see, I believe that the psychoanalytic approach should be conceived as an outfit that is tailor-made.

The expectation that trainee analysts have, and which I too had in my day, is to build up a systematic structure of theories and knowledge to understand and confidently keep one's bearings in clinical work. Unfortunately, however, psychoanalytic knowledge derives from and constantly enriches itself through analytic practice, the efficiency of which is always being enhanced. Having valid knowledge constantly is not possible. Frequently, even when an analyst has acquired considerable competence, he wonders at his not knowing something that comes up in a session and at how his vision never stops expanding.

From this viewpoint, it is clear that there is no general psychoanalytic theory, or, rather, there is no single explanatory theory that helps us understand the many-sidedness of clinical experience. There are, however, hypotheses that can be helpful when applied to specific psychopathological domains. In psychoanalysis, as in any science, eternal truths do not exist, and it would certainly be a serious mistake to consider Freud's texts as sacred, despite their needing to be read and then compared to and integrated with what has followed.

CHAPTER 1

On the specific nature of psychoanalysis

For some years now, appeals have been made periodically to psychoanalysis to integrate its wealth of knowledge with that of other disciplines, evolutionary biology and neuroscience in particular, in order to avoid cultural isolation.

On this matter, I would like to reflect on the difference between comparing psychoanalysis with other disciplines on the one hand, and its possible integration with them on the other. I believe that, whereas a comparison with other disciplines is necessary and useful, its integration with them is neither useful nor possible, given that psychoanalysis has its own specific epistemology.

For example, cognitive science and neuroscience both use objective observational methods, whereas psychoanalysis is a subjective discipline in which the subject observes himself as he operates, thinks, and feels emotions. Specific to psychoanalysis is its examination of unconscious life, which can only be done through introspection. In unconscious life, although there are experiences that cannot be consciously observed, they can subsequently be recognised indirectly.

That subjectivity is a specific element of the psychoanalytic method implies a series of limits, one of which is insufficient validation of therapeutic outcomes, given that psychoanalysis does not use the direct observational experimental method employed by the natural sciences. Indeed, Freud founded psychoanalysis on an intensive study of single cases, and analytic clinical work developed out of isolated clinical cases whose comparison would have served no purpose. For this reason, the specific nature of psychoanalysis raises a series of methodological issues for scholars from other disciplines.

That said, recently, groups of psychoanalysts have worked to identify objective research methods for change that is obtained in psychoanalytic therapies. We must ask ourselves, though, whether this attempt to render the therapeutic effect quantifiable risks losing partial sight of the specific element of psychoanalysis. Personally, I have my doubts about being able to objectivise (as in the natural sciences) movements that occur in the analytic relationship. How is it possible to give an 'objective' edge to subjective transformations? What is gained in quantity may be lost in quality. Methods that use objective parameters find it difficult to capture the single individual's specific journey, his individual development, which is wealth belonging solely to the analyst and analysand.

In clinical work, the analyst's task is to infer a link between a set of sensory data, images, memories, and emotions that formerly were neither linked nor meaningful. This work bears a similarity to mental operations carried out by any kind of intuitive scientist. In the natural sciences, too, inferences are needed that bear similarities to those made by a psychoanalyst when seeking to understand his own and others' mental functioning. There is, however, a substantial difference between the mental work of the experimental scientist and intuitive work by the psychoanalyst: the former starts with a hypothesis that needs experimental confirmation (and replicability is crucial in order to confirm the hypothesis); the latter, however, tries to solve a problem through mental work that is unique, personal, and not replicable.

Yet another difference lies in the fact that a natural scientist works with an external object, whereas a psychoanalyst considers the person's inner world. Psychoanalysis concerns itself with objects such as emotions, feelings, thoughts, memories, and identity (that which we psychoanalysts call psychic reality); these constitute immaterial but real entities that need to be studied but not nullified or 'reified' because of their nature.

In scientific language, the term *subjective* takes on the meaning of personal or individual, and even opining or being limited to a single individual's particular viewpoint. The subjective view is therefore not scientific. From a psychoanalytic perspective, subjective instead means the personal world, a person's specific identity and his relationship with affects and the world.

The ambition of the psychoanalytic method is to formulate a language that enables the subjective experience, fleeting and elusive as it is, to be perceived, described, and communicated using the same clearness with which we perceive natural reality. Unlike other psychology disciplines that use the objective method, psychoanalysis avails itself of procedures based solely on the intuitive imagination of one's own and others' mental processes.

On the specific nature of psychoanalysis

From this perspective, it is possible to see not only analogies but also differences between psychoanalysis and other disciplines that study the mind. I should like to make a brief reference here to neuroscience, whose development over recent decades has been significant, leading to important cognitive contributions that cannot be ignored. Although the focus of both psychoanalysis and neuroscience is unconscious mechanisms that regulate mental growth, learning, and emotions, a gap that cannot be easily bridged divides them. In fact, as I have just argued, the substantial difference between the natural sciences and psychoanalysis is that the former is in search of objective truths that can be tested via shared observation, whereas the latter studies personal truth, which is not universal but experienced through subjective intuition.

From this difference derives the problem of how psychoanalytic knowledge can be shared with and transmitted to those who do not take part in this process. To the non-followers, most psychoanalytic inferences seem random, if not altogether suspicious. What we have here is the problem philosophers refer to as logical justification (which, according to Popper, is the weak spot of psychoanalysis). For the natural sciences, data obtained by inference are replicable, shareable, and verifiable. Psychoanalytic inference, unlike that of mathematics or science, can be shared only by the subject that can recognise it in himself or perceive it through his effort to identify with another. This knowledge is mutable not only because that particular associative thread, that story, or that emotional truth holds a certain value for a particular individual, but also because of the speed and 'volatility' of psychic and emotional experiences.

Like other scientific methods that start from observed data to arrive at general laws, psychoanalysis too sets aside subjective experience to build theoretical models that give meaning to single observations: its models serve to bring each piece of experimental data within a framework. During this stage, following clinical work, psychoanalysis builds its models and theories to generalise concordant experiences and to provide explanatory hypotheses on mental functioning. Some models are short-lived, whereas others, which are continually validated and can express general truths, are destined to remain.

One complex aspect of analytic intuitions is that in order to be validated, an experimental area is needed, that is, the analytic setting, not so much in the sense of a formal frame (couch, times, payment), but a mental environment suited to receiving and registering unconscious psychic and emotional facts.

Without this area, a psychoanalyst would find himself in the same conditions as an atomic physicist wanting to study subatomic particles without a particle accelerator. Inside this mental setting, psychic facts take on value and meaning through a form of personal and subjective recognition, a procedure that eludes any external comparison, but which should not be misunderstood as an arbitrary act or an absence of recognisable rules. Indeed, in analytic practice, there are complex and sophisticated rules and trajectories that lead to discoveries. The analytic experience is a method for gaining knowledge of psychic realities which *employs emotional-intuitive functions* connected to the self-observation of one's mental and emotional processes. These functions are unconscious and potentially present in every human being.

For this reason, psychoanalysis can be considered a scientific discipline with *a specific epistemological status*, whose area of research includes the study of the roots of thought itself. The unconscious, comprising a set of functions outside awareness, memories, emotional awareness, and intersubjective and relational experience, gives us a glimpse at how functions outside awareness operate, functions that are extremely important for the development of the mind.

CHAPTER 2

Making a diagnosis in psychoanalysis

To speak of diagnosis in psychoanalysis can give rise to misunderstandings which need to be looked at and clarified.

In medicine, it is fundamental to place a disorder within a diagnosis, since only an exact definition of clinical features can result in an adequate therapeutic response.

In psychoanalysis, a medical-type diagnosis would not be useful, as the analyst does not simply want to 'treat' or eradicate a 'disease', but address the analysand's development potential, without being concerned in the first instance about concurrent symptoms. Given the psychic life complexities of any individual who begins therapy, a diagnostic intention alone, aside from being objectifying, would also be misleading.

However, in psychoanalytic practice, we cannot proceed in uncertainty, using solely our intuition; the analyst must also formulate hypotheses and have reference points in order to carry his work forward. On meeting for the first time a person who has requested psychoanalytic help, the analyst cannot not contemplate formulating a general framework.

For example, it is extremely important to understand whether the analysand is suffering from a neurotic condition or a psychotic disorder.

In the latter case, the psychoanalyst knows he cannot treat the patient as he would a neurotic patient. With a psychotic patient, cautiousness is needed on the one hand and boldness on the other. Cautiousness is needed because the psychotic patient is unable to use intuitive thought, and therefore many psychoanalytic interventions could be either altered or captured in delusional distortions, through which the patient perceives reality. And boldness is needed because the patient, right from the very beginning, wants the analyst to understand his specific functioning related to his specific mental state.

Therefore, a psychoanalyst, as he listens to the patient, intends not to make a medical-type diagnosis but to infer the mental functioning that lies behind that patient's particular type of clinical manifestation.

Even when we find ourselves dealing with types of suffering that are apparently limited to a single symptom, we must not focus only on that particular symptom and how it manifests. For example, if a psychoanalyst interviews a patient who presents with panic attacks, it is important to ask oneself what the underlying personality structure is, and which defence collapse led to that kind of disorder. Panic could be a symptom of relational suffering (the loss of someone who lent support), or the manifestation of a crisis connected to going from one stage in life to another (a midlife crisis): both situations involve personal identity problems and an existential crisis that require a change in perspective and a more suitable arrangement for the future.

Being understood within one's own subjective experience is what a patient first and foremost asks of the analyst, who is called upon to understand the complexity of that individual's inner world.

From the very start, the analyst must identify how the patient relates to his surrounding world and those in it. Psychoanalytic understanding, or, rather, the response the analyst gives to the patient's first communications, is the base the analytic relationship will be built on, a bond that is destined to support and last the length of the therapeutic path.

The analyst has this understanding because he is able to think and infer according to *similarity* and *difference*. Having an accurate sense of his own identity (his values, beliefs, and inner world), he tries to be aware of how his interlocutor subjectively perceives reality. From this difference, he can then understand how to usefully proceed with the analytic work.

Psychoanalytic competence

Psychoanalytic competence is rooted in the analyst's ability to put himself *in the shoes of another* who is different from him, that is, to infer the state of mind of his interlocutor, who can have a different vision, even an opposite vision, of the world from his, but who is unable to communicate this explicitly. From this constant comparison between the analyst's perception and the patient's, intuitions begin to form of the way the analysand deals with (or avoids) problems that come his way.

But this *ability* to empathically perceive the *similarity and difference* of the other's state of mind is not enough; one also needs to infer how the reasons for his state of mind began long before, often in childhood. One of Freud's major intuitions is that early childhood experiences are fundamental to structuring the causes for unhappiness in adult life, or, on the contrary, to guaranteeing our existence a moderate degree of serenity.

Freud's primitive intuition became more helpful and articulated when he understood that unresolved childhood conflicts could be transferred onto the figure of the analyst, and that in this new relationship, it was possible to modify and transform them.

Starting from these considerations, it is important that from the very beginning, the analyst can perceive the quality of the patient's original objects, and sense what his traumatic emotional history may have been.

To help the patient develop an ability to cope with life circumstances (loss, grief, and being able to maintain meaningful relationships), we cannot disregard his emotional history. By emotional history, I do not mean a reconstruction of past events, which assumes a sort of shared and verified objectivity (we know the extent to which memory can be flawed and the character of past objects distorted by conflicts and past and present emotions); what I do mean is intuitive work carried out by the analyst to reach explanatory hypotheses.

The patient's history does not therefore coincide with a reconstruction of events or the character of primary objects, but with recovering emotions that the patient necessarily had to change or cancel from his conscious memory.

Psychoanalysis subscribes to a model of emotional and psychological development that takes into consideration the complexity of both subjective and objective variables which condition the development of the mind.

By variables, I mean those elements that do not depend solely on adequate or distorted responses from primary objects, but also on a child's subjective inclination to create defences and psychopathological structures that, despite originating in emotional trauma, mark development that is largely independent of the original environmental influence over time.

An extreme example would be that of a child whose anxiety manifestations indicate his emotionally unavailable mother's lack of attention. Consequently, he tries to enter a psychic withdrawal, where body fantasies that are capable of creating a state of mental excitement go on to take the place of dependence on a human object, dependence that is required for development.

Since the analyst encounters these facts on a daily basis, he is well aware of them; he is also equipped with a model of the mind's mental development, a theory of the mind, that is based on an abundance of observed data. From this knowledge, he can build hypotheses on the patient's history that are unconnected to evidence and which even the patient cannot provide.

Naturally, much attention is needed when the patient recalls the traumatic nature of past objects. Freud himself ran up against theoretical errors by paying too much attention to the narration of his patients' traumas. Childhood traumatic events, which have their historical objectivity, can frequently be used to maintain a victimistic psychic pattern that justifies constantly exercising vindictiveness and sadomasochistic excitement.

When there have been childhood traumas, it is important to be able to discern the patient's attempt to involve the analyst in his victim mentality perspective from a more complex situation in which the patient is unaware of any emotional trauma or its nature. In some cases, the trauma may have been so powerful that the traumatic event cannot be remembered, or perhaps the child's response was to create defences or psychopathological constructions that left no space for experienced reality.

An intuitive object

My viewpoint stems from acknowledging that in order to grow, we need the mind of another we can go to with our queries, anxieties, wishes, and needs. Repeatedly encountering this experience and having meaning given back to our projections permits the introjection of an object that is capable of intuiting and emotionally understanding us. Patients who come to us lack this object and are therefore unable to understand why they are suffering. The real trauma is having introjected an object that does not understand emotions and deprives psychic life of any meaning.

From this viewpoint, psychoanalytic therapy could be defined as an experience which can develop in the patient the emotional understanding function that the primary object either lacked or distorted. In some cases, perverse, borderline, or psychotic, for instance, this function cannot develop until psychic space is rid of pathological structures that occupy it.

To understand and help the patient, we use the tool of emotional intuition; analytic interpretation is therapeutic because it provides experience with meaning and helps the patient not only to understand in general terms but also to understand himself emotionally.

We understand not only because we interpret, referring to something else symbolically, but also because we are able to put ourselves in the patient's shoes and reach him empathically in his present and past. We interpret to provide the patient with real and emotional understanding of his psychic experience.

Analytic interpretation, that is, what the analyst communicates via his *intuitive work*, is useful to the patient because it allows him to experience an object that can think emotionally, and then gradually introject this function.

CHAPTER 3

The significance of history

One of the many analysts who appreciated the value of reconstructing the past for therapeutic purposes was Eric Brenman, who stated:

> To my mind, knowing his background provides him with a sense of continuity and meaning. Only if he feels he belongs can he achieve his own identity. Reconstruction is of value as a means of rediscovering roots, past objects and lost parts of the self. (Brenman, 2006, p. 11)

Yet another assertion by this same author regards the credibility of the reconstruction:

> Distortion of the truth in the construction of the part played by environment or instincts occurs at the deepest levels and may be influenced by the biases and pathology of both analyst and patient. The reshaping of the truth may be not only the current practice of the patient, but a repetition of the past. (Brenman, 2006, p. 12)

Brenman underlined that reconstruction of the past can differ according to the individual's viewpoint. For example, in the reconstruction of the Oedipus myth, there can be a drive version or a traumatic version of the same story. According to the first, Oedipus kills his father because he wants to possess his mother; according to the second, it is because the parents abandoned their son. As has been rightly observed, it is difficult to imagine that Oedipus was endowed with good enough objects enabling him to deal with his oedipal complex.

In the wake of Freud, who assumed that it was possible to arrive at the truth of childhood matters, the position of most analysts is that the transference, in it being a repetition of the past, can guarantee the veracity of the childhood event. Other analysts (Spence, 1982; Schafer, 1983) instead theorise that there can be no reconstruction of historical truth, the only truth being narrative truth.

Peculiar to psychoanalysis is the hypothesis that relationships with objects who took care of us in childhood are fundamental to our development and our future life. The quality of responses we received during the first part of our life forms the basis of our subsequent emotional disposition.

Insight into and emotional understanding of the past, which become possible at a certain point in the analysis, show that the analysand's receptive empathy has broadened, and the wealth he has acquired is able to illuminate the past. It is not the memory that is recovered, but the ability to remember and integrate.

Reaching a truth about one's personal past, in my opinion, allows what was made unconscious because of defences, self-idealisation, or the projection of responsibility onto original objects to be restored, and split-off and lost parts of the self to be recovered.

To understand the patient's difficulties, I believe it is important to reconstruct his history and, given that memory can be distorted by present conflicts and emotions, the analyst must formulate meaningful hypotheses that, via the reconstruction of interaction with the original objects, help to understand the precarious equilibrium of the present. Through his intuitive work centred on the patient's past, the analyst can formulate hypotheses capable of explaining the possible distortion of emotional development and the traumatic nature of early childhood experiences.

Modell (1999) makes a distinction between a single traumatic experience (for instance, that reconstructed by Freud in 'Wolf Man') and repeated emotional experiences of absent maternal participation; he reminds us, moreover, of how infant research's direct observation has confirmed that at ten months of age, the emotional response of children whose mothers are depressed has already organised itself differently from that of children with normal mothers (Tronick, 1989; Beebe, Lachmann, & Jaffe, 1997). I shall not dwell here on the definition and consequences of trauma, but only underline the subjective element that accompanies it in its pathogenic effects.

Reconstructive hypotheses

I am convinced that we can begin to reconstruct the past right from the first encounter while hypothesising, that is, much sooner than the transference manifests. From the very first interviews, I tend to listen to the narration of the patient's story and his problems, and, at the same time, use my analytic receptiveness to sense which primary objects the patient had and whether his parents were able to develop his person, or, on the contrary, to inhibit its development. In other words, I formulate inside myself the questions that enable me to hypothesise what, both inner or outer, was capable of blocking or distorting his emotional development and his real identity.

I try to reconstruct intuitively the patient's emotional path, placing side by side what he consciously remembers and what his present state of difficulty is. From the *gap between his narrative and his insight*, I can develop a hypothesis on what he *does not know* about his past, his original objects, and his own mental functioning.

By formulating these reconstructive hypotheses, one can also intuit early on several possible transference dynamics and anxieties that may later emerge in the analytic relationship. Naturally, any reference made to the past by the analyst must be exact and timely and never used as a defence against conflicts or turbulence in the analytic relationship.

Once formulated, these hypotheses can be modified and integrated with other elements that will emerge over the course of the analytic process, during which the analysand will move in original ways and be capable of surprising the analyst, who must then let his hypotheses go and open his mind up towards the new and unknown.

If the analyst has been able to gather inside and put to good use the patient's history of emotional development and the pathogenic interaction with the primary object, which will re-emerge in analysis as the transference becomes established, an adequate response from him will be elicited more easily.

As can be seen, my point of view differs from those colleagues (among the many is Betty Joseph, 1985) who believe that reconstructing childhood history is only of help at a much later stage in the analysis. Naturally, we can only communicate our hypotheses to the patient when he is able to understand them, but there is no general rule to apply to all cases. The analyst can evaluate when the best moment arrives by taking into account the patient's personality and his ability to understand, which is unconnected to the duration of the analysis.

What is the importance of reconstructing the past for therapeutic purposes? Can we really think that, when the past is reintegrated, the therapeutic purpose has been accomplished? How can a relationship be formed that will produce new developments?

Recovering the past

Traditionally, it was believed that the crux of analytic work lay in transference interpretations and reconstructing the past. This view got its start from the Freudian vision of neurosis, which sees its origins in repressed infantile conflict that is reproduced in the transference during treatment.

My view is that interpreting the transference and reconstructing the past are necessary steps, but alone are not enough. For a bond of dependence oriented at the development of mental growth, we must count on the *analytic relationship*, a concept I shall consider in more detail further ahead.

Can the past actually be recovered in all cases?

When we treat neurotic patients, the experience of the emotional trauma is present in unconscious awareness, and it is therefore destined to emerge during analytic work. In more severe cases, such as borderline conditions, difficult childhood experiences distort personality development and favour the construction of pathological structures that wipe out the memory of the traumatic experience. A more complex path is therefore necessary here, since the link between psychopathology and trauma is more concealed and indirect.

To answer the question of whether reconstructing the past is possible with a particular patient, we can say 'yes' only for those cases in which there is an unconscious that has associative memory and can think metaphorically. These unconscious functions, largely active in the neurotic patient, are badly deteriorated, if not totally absent, in borderline and psychotic patients.

Research in the field of developmental psychology and attachment theory have highlighted the importance of early interactions between mother and child during his first months of life for the organisation of the self, interactions that occur at a pre-symbolic and a preverbal level. Mimetic, visual, and verbal exchanges are considered essential for the formation of the very first elements that enable a child to develop his emotional world and his ability to understand the meaning of relationships. Among the many contributions within this contemporary overview, I shall cite Beebe et al. (1997), who have cast light on early interactive structures that originate in the ways a mother and child communicate emotionally during the first year of the child's life, before his first words.

Over the course of pathological processes and repeated emotional traumas from which borderline states seem to have their start, unconscious functions undergo a series of transformations, such that their intrapsychic and relational communication function gets completely wiped out.

If we compare the emotional unconscious to a language, then that language in neurosis, which allows us to read the past, is preserved and just needs to be better articulated to become comprehensible. In the case of a borderline patient, we find ourselves facing a civilisation whose evolution towards language, or, rather, towards the possibility of structuring and understanding one's history, did not take place; there is no understandable language at our disposal because that ability to narrate and communicate simply is not there. A similar distortion occurs in psychosis, where a communicative structure such as the unconscious is constantly under attack from a constructed isolated and grandiose world where receptive and communicative channels of psychic reality have been destroyed.

This state of affairs makes not only therapy but also the reconstruction of the past extremely problematic. We can therefore only reach it hypothetically amid the patient's constant difficulty to acquire and integrate it into his inner world.

CHAPTER 4

Psychoanalytic theories

As I mentioned earlier, theoretical models have grown in number as psychoanalytic thought has developed; even psychoanalytic concepts have acquired new meanings depending on the theoretical context in which they are placed. And if we examine psychoanalytic literature historically, we can see that some particularly prominent concepts in the past have disappeared altogether today, some new ones have appeared, and the meaning of other existing concepts has undergone change.

In this chapter, I shall present three theories: the Freudian psychosexual theory, Melanie Klein's object relations theory, which was then further developed by Bion, and intersubjective systems theory. I have chosen these three theories to show the differences between them and some consequences on a clinical level that this leads to.

Psychosexual theory

Freud's ability to formulate increasingly complex theories on the psychic apparatus and integrate them into previous theories is one of the qualities of his thought.

As we know, some of the first cases Freud treated analytically were outside his medical practice, at the patient's home; this was so with Anna O., Breuer and Freud's famous patient, who christened the analytic method the 'talking cure'.

Not until later was the psychoanalytic setting introduced, that is, the formal tool of psychological therapy: a spatial environment (patient and analyst always meet in the same place) and set times (a certain number of weekly sessions at a certain time are arranged).

Using the couch deserves a separate mention. This facilitates an almost total exclusion of external sensory stimuli and consequently more attentive communication between patient and analyst. The formal setting (i.e. those constant features regarding the time and place of the therapy) has remained the same since Freud's day, whereas the analyst's mental setting (i.e. his selective attention regarding the patient and the analytic relationship) has undergone important transformations over the years.

According to psychosexual theory, repressing sexuality and one's childhood past are at the root of neurotic suffering. Healing occurs by disclosing and understanding Freudian slips, dreams, and the transference, which allow past historical truth and psychic reality to be reconstructed.

Freudian analytic technique involves the analyst interpreting repressed content with tools deriving from the discovery of dream dynamics (latent and manifest content). In its being repressed, the unconscious conflict produces the symptom, and interpretation must make conflict content emerge. Since the transference takes the analytic relationship back to early childhood experiences, analysing it is of crucial importance. Material the patient provides is a text whose hidden meaning needs to be interpreted to make it manifest. Freudian technique, moreover, tends to mitigate the severity of the superego by transforming archaic unconscious fantasies.

One of the cornerstones of psychosexual theory lies in the analysis of sexuality, whose conceptualisation changed over the developmental course of Freudian thought. We can identify three periods that set out three theories of the psychic apparatus, which correspond in part to three subsequent theoretical viewpoints on sexuality.

In the *first period* (1882–1895), resulting in *Studies on Hysteria* (1895d), Freud identified the pathogenic agent of neurosis in sexuality, and theorised its traumatic aetiology (which he then modified). As we shall see more clearly in the following chapters, he distinguished between actual neuroses, caused by a dysfunction in the sexual charge, and psychoneuroses. Sexuality that Freud referred to in that period belonged to conventional language, that is, it was a repressed sexual and romantic wish.

In the *second period*, the aetiological hypothesis of neurosis involved a general theory of the individual's development. Sexuality changed from the common meaning of sexual love to a 'psychoanalytic', metaphoric, and metapsychological meaning. Psychosexuality, expressed in *Three Essays on the Theory of Sexuality* (1905d), derived from a modification to two types of parameter: the first was the area and the extension of sexuality, and the second its qualitative and conceptual transformation. In harmony with the primacy of the pleasure principle, Freud extended sexuality to include every form of bodily pleasure. All sensory forms of pleasure were primitive components of the *libido*: the sensory pleasure of a nursling's sucking was an expression of sexuality.

Sexuality remained intimately linked to the energy model. Freud (1909b) explained that in obsessive neurosis, the very thought process could be sexualised and a repetitive line of ideas experienced as a replacement for sexual satisfaction. Psychotic patients' inability to cope with the large quantity of instinctual energy that is freed up during the illness, as in the case of Schreber, would result in a part of this energy being sexualised.

Perverse sexuality was nothing other than a variant of sexuality, that is, the resulting distortion of libidinal development and ego maturity that originated in a difficulty to overcome normal stages of libidinal organisation. The perverse individual remained anchored to a type of pregenital sexuality.

The *third period* coincided with a shift in 1920: sexuality, set against the death drive, was a positive love force that created ties and opposed death. It was no longer a primitive and aggressive force but Eros in a constant struggle with Thanatos.

I feel it is important to underline that in the progressive modulation of Freudian theory, sexuality was always a single concept: its expressions varied, it had aggressive or tender components, and it could be in opposition or tied to the death instinct, but it was always within a unitary theory.

Attempts to reach a general understanding of psychic disorder drove Freud to advance several classifications of mental illnesses; these were hypotheses that he himself changed over the course of his work and which were influenced by the greater or lesser sophisticated theory that he was developing at a particular time. He distinguished between the *transference neuroses*, where the libido is free and can be transferred to objects, and the *narcissistic neuroses*, in which there is a withdrawal of libido from objects and consequent difficulty in forming a transference.

The disorder or illness is seen in Freudian theory as regression to or a developmental arrest at a stage of primitive organisation; *fixation points* and *regression* are important concepts.

According to Freud, in neurosis, the libido regressed to a primitive stage of organisation. This implied that every neurosis had its specific fixation point, and its form was determined by the specific stage in which psychosexual developmental arrest occurred.

What is interesting in Abraham's (1924) paper is his correlation between psychosexual stages and corresponding levels of object relations. This author drew up a general table to facilitate envisaging all the developmental stages, object love, and various forms of neurotic suffering matched to specific forms of disorders found in clinical work.

Object relations theory

Melanie Klein's starting point was the role of anxiety in emotional development: the child is prey to sadistic phantasies in relation to the maternal body, and from these his persecutory anxieties get their start. The primitive nature of object organisation is prominent in Klein's theory, but the action of a traumatic factor not so much: primitive oral sadism produces phantasies of attacking and devouring the love object.

To defend oneself from excessive aggressiveness and sadism, numerous defences are mobilised, such as splitting, denial, idealisation, and many forms of identification. Idealisation, for instance, enables the child to defend himself against persecutory fear, but at the same time, it increases his omnipotent desire to have an inexhaustible breast that is always available.

Confronted with primary destructiveness (which later coincided with envy), guilt and wanting reparation are generated. The therapeutic process entailed gaining awareness of the love–hate conflict that then mobilised attempts at reparation in the depressive position. Interpreting destructiveness served to make the patient aware of his splitting and projecting, and it was therefore necessary in order to integrate his personality.

One of Klein's (1946) most original contributions was the concept of parts of the self being split off and projected into the object, that is, *projective identification*, a process which leads to confusion between the self and the object. Improvement in therapy is when parts of the patient's projected personality are reintegrated.

Klein described two fundamental moments in psychic development: the paranoid–schizoid position and the depressive position. The former is characterised by a tendency to react aggressively to frustration, without discerning whether such is intentional or inevitable. In other words, the child hates his mother when she does not protect him from frustration, whereas he loves her when she gratifies him. In the depressive position, the child allows his mother to be a separate person with her own needs and desires, and he wishes to repair his past aggressiveness.

Whereas, for Freud, the objective of therapy was reached when the infantile complex (oedipal) was overcome, for Klein, healing was through reparation that the patient carried out in relation to the object that had been attacked and destroyed in phantasy. Rather than aiming to reconstruct the patient's history, interpretation principally concerned the relationship between the patient and the analyst.

For Freud, in the transference, the analyst represented a figure from childhood, which therefore allowed the past to be reconstructed; in Kleinian technique, however, the analyst became the recipient of projections of the patient's split-off parts. In this kind of approach, the 'here and now' is more important than the reconstruction of the past. In Kleinian technique, a systematic analysis of the transference, that is, the projection of the patient's split-off parts, helps the patient to recover an integrated image of himself in which libidinal aspects override destructive components. This can only happen when split-off parts of the self, which are unconscious and contain envy, have been experienced as negative and reparation processes begin to be active.

Klein's contributions prompted analytic therapy for psychosis using a setting similar to that used for neurotic patients. Through the concept of pathological projective identification, a typically psychotic mechanism, it was possible to explain confusional states in this kind of patient. According to Klein, psychotic patients lose their boundaries and their individuality because they would like to omnipotently take possession of the object's personality, which they perceive as desirable and therefore envied.

Bionian theory

In Bionian theory (the last period), the concept of container is essential. Sadistic attacks and destructive fantasies are such not only because of the primitive drive (Abraham), or the strength of the death instinct (Klein), but a deficiency in maternal containment. With Bion, not only the theory of mental illness but also the function of the analyst and analytic technique underwent change. Therapeutic capacity was achieved through receiving, understanding, and returning anxieties in a form that the patient could assimilate.

In Bion's vision, the child plunges into nameless dread when his mother is unable to receive, transform, and return his projective identifications. This process is at the root of all distortions and breakdowns in the adult personality. Not only might it be that the mother does not receive the child's projective identifications, but she can even project her own anxieties into the child, using him as a container. The container–contained dynamic is re-actualised in the transference and the countertransference. Whereas Klein had excluded using the countertransference for therapeutic purposes, Bion valued its use and defined its nature and therapeutic function: the mother and the analyst respond to the child's/patient's projective identifications using their emotional intuition (reverie) to dispel the distressing content of the experience. The importance of the countertransference lies in the analytic object being able to respond to the patient's conscious or unconscious requests in terms of emotional development.

Intersubjective systems theory

I shall now consider intersubjective systems theory, which is representative of other theories in contemporary psychoanalysis. These theories favour the quality of the patient/analyst relationship, removing from the foreground, if not altogether excluding, the importance of history, defences, and psychopathological constructions that the analysand is a carrier of. In my opinion, this brings with it the risk of oversimplifying the therapeutic course and narrowing the clinical horizon.

Intersubjective systems theory is the result of contributions by a group of analysts from the United States, who were inspired by several of Kohut's intuitions and who enriched their approach with attachment theory.

Stolorow, Atwood, and Brandchaft (1994) define their theory as originating in a model directed at conceptualising the organisation of personal experience and its vicissitudes within an intersubjective system of behaviour. Their conceptualisation differs from other psychoanalytic theories in that it does not set out specific psychic contents (such as the Oedipus complex, the paranoid–schizoid position, separation–individuation conflicts, mirroring and idealisation needs, etc.), which are universally considered as relevant in personality development and pathogenesis. Organising principles derive from the concept of intersubjectivity and they operate in the area of the *pre-reflective unconscious*, representing an alternative to the concept of the drive-based unconscious fantasy. It is these unconscious organising principles, produced within the child–attachment figure system intersection, that constitute the foundations of personality development and represent the core of psychoanalytic investigation and interpretation.

According to this theory, pathology is a consequence of the parental figures having been unable to understand and modulate the child's emotional states, thus determining the future development of *defence-based obstructed affective states*. This 'defensive sequestering' represents a source of resistance to the analytic treatment, which can vary depending on the patient's perception of the extent of the analyst's receptiveness.

This perspective proposes a 'traumatic' model, in which what is meant by trauma is the failed affective and emotional response of early relational objects; the trauma leads to withdrawal, or, rather, to the 'sequestering' of conscious emotional experiences that are able to be experienced within relationships.

Intersubjective theorising recalls Kohut's perspective on the selfobject as an unconscious organiser of primitive experiences needed for growth.

Authors belonging to this group contend that in the analytic process, progress derives from moments of *intersubjective joining* (when the organising principles of the patient's experience correspond to the basic psychic life patterns of the analyst, whose response will then be congruous with the analysand's requests); and regression derives from moments of *intersubjective disjoining* (when the analyst gathers together the patient's material in patterns that greatly alter its meaning).

Even if intersubjective disjoining were to provoke an impasse, the patient would continue to communicate with the analyst in order to reactivate those patterns that allow new organising principles to start up.

To recapitulate, therapy must be taken forward with moments of intersubjective joining predominating; when disjoining prevails, a therapeutic impasse is encountered and, consequently, a halt to the analytic process. Even if we consider intersubjective joining as indispensable for the continuation of the analytic process, we must also consider that intersubjective theory says little about the complexity of the patient's inner world and his psychopathology. Not only are all conscious and unconscious dynamics abolished in this model, but the entire psychopathology too.

CHAPTER 5

The unconscious and emotional reality

This chapter considers several issues regarding the epistemological status of the unconscious and a broadening of perspectives, starting from Freud's early intuitions. I shall begin with the premise that the unconscious is not a unitary entity; theoretical models that have succeeded one another throughout the development of psychoanalytic thought often refer to various forms of the unconscious, describable as different functions of the mind.

In short, we may say that psychoanalysis has moved away from the original energy-drive concept of the unconscious, favouring instead the emotional-cognitive aspect at the expense of the animal, drive, and sexual legacy suggested not univocally by Freud.

Sigmund Freud

The Freudian unconscious is a tank of primitive instincts and unspeakable wishes, of a personal and a phylogenetic past, but not only. By describing the unconscious function of understanding and receiving, Freud (1912b) was also speaking of the analyst's unconscious as a receptive organ that allows contact to be made with the patient's unconscious.

Later (1923b), he stated that the organ designated to consciousness, the ego, was partly unconscious—not preconscious, but an unrepressed unconscious.

In this case, Freud anticipated some modern conceptions of unconscious parts of emotional perception and the unconscious roots of the self. Despite having underlined the highly developed unconscious functions of emotional communication, Freud did not develop these intuitions in depth.

Stressed more in analytic theory was the repressed unconscious, which is anchored to our animal inheritance and can be found in *Civilization and its Discontents* (1930a), where human unhappiness is considered as an inevitable consequence of the irreconcilable tension between nature and culture.

Melanie Klein

Melanie Klein, as we know, introduced two important new concepts: the notion of unconscious phantasy and, alongside repression, the concept of the splitting of the object and subsequently splitting and projection (projective identification). Unconscious phantasy is different from unconscious representation: in addition to being the psychic representative of the drive, it is also the mental representation of physical perceptions (interpreted as relations between objects), corresponding anxieties, and defences. In the unconscious conceptualised by Klein, the unconscious is broadened to the bi-personal field, spatial metaphor being emphasised: a projection that occurs inside another person changes the perception of the subject who projects, and it distorts the perception of the object who receives the projection.

Wilfred Bion

In Bion's thought, the unconscious loses its ontic meaning of place. It is no longer a space where repressed content can be deposited, but a function of the mind, an imaginative instrument that transforms sensory experience into thought. In fact, for Bion, 'thinking' coincided with being able to 'dream'.

The dream, like the unconscious, is an intrapsychic and relational communication and not a construction that needs to be interpreted. It is a function that fashions and registers emotions, a daytime activity that is always active. Through the dream, the unconscious provides symbolic and imaginative replenishment that transforms sensory experience into thought; it metabolises psychic experiences, and when this function is inadequate or fails, the mind is prevented from producing thoughts (semi-permeable membrane and alpha function).

The contrast is no longer between the repressed unconscious (Freud) or splitting (Klein) and consciousness, but between the awake state and sleep, between consciousness inside or outside awareness.

Due to his theory of thoughts without a thinker, the patient may be conscious but not aware. In psychotic states, thoughts have no thinker because deterioration of the alpha function has occurred.

The relational unconscious

The relational aspect of unconscious functions is the most creative part of contemporary psychoanalysis, starting from various authors such as Winnicott (with his concepts of potential space of the self and the true self), Kohut, Bollas, relational analysts, and intersubjective analysts.

Bollas (1987, 1992) speaks of an *existential memory* and *unthought known* to describe a series of events that escape representation, that is, memory outside awareness that we all have. Bollas contends that children internalise the 'maternal idiom' of care, which refers to a complex way of being and relating, in other words, a part of the psyche that lives in a world without words. Bollas' conceptualisation can be likened to the idea of implicit memory, a memory that contains all those events that cannot be recollected as they happened at too early an age and are not conveyed by conscious representations but do, however, shape individual growth.

Stolorow and Atwood (1992), too, broaden the concept of the unconscious to include that part of personal history which, never having been confirmed, cannot become experience of which the individual is aware. According to these authors, we make unconscious not only what is omnipotent and destructive, but also what is good and constructive when it is in conflict with our caregiver's vision; most of our infantile awareness and 'wisdom' is thus made unconscious and unavailable.

Donna Orange (1998) calls 'emotional memory' a function that can help explain why the therapeutic process is much more complex than the simple formula from the theory of repression and resistance of 'making the unconscious conscious'. Emotional memory remains incorporated in an individual's organising principles, maintaining its power until new experiences take shape. According to this author, the analytic bond and the mutual relationship of research and understanding open the way to new emotional memories, new stories, and new opportunities.

These hypotheses help us to understand how infantile intersubjective experience is introjected and that the environmental response plays a decisive role. Through projection and the distortion of the caregiving primary object, we introject prohibitions and threats that endorse 'not knowing' (Bion's -K), that is, blind spots of the mind.

It is along this line of thought that studies by Mauro Mancia (2004) developed, and for whom the discovery of a double memory system (explicit and implicit) led to the hypothesis of a double organisation of the unconscious: one part is connected to *explicit* memory, which makes the process of repression possible, and another to *implicit* memory, which does not concern repression (unrepressed unconscious), but operates in our mind throughout our whole life, influencing affects, emotions, and behaviours without us having any memory, consciousness, or awareness of it. Mancia assigned a broad area to the unrepressed unconscious, ranging from psychopathological patterns originating in relational trauma to 'formal' communicative means that characterise each single patient's transference. Specifically, voice and language convey affects and emotions that connect back to early experience with the mother and the environment. These means constitute the 'musical dimension' of the transference.

From this short review, we can see how the analyst's attention has shifted away from an unconscious that operates according to repression towards an unconscious that is implicit and outside awareness.

The picture of unconscious functions that emerges from contemporary psychoanalysis is so innovatory that it needs to be compared with the pre-existing 'psychoanalytic system' and any necessary integrations then effectuated.

Emphasis has now moved away from the 'repressed' to the 'not yet represented', from 'discovered' to 'created', from patient to analyst, and from the analyst's knowledge to his emotional receptiveness and respect for the patient's verbal and nonverbal communication.

Modern visions of the emotional unconscious have opened up new perspectives in therapeutic work, which now takes the shape of a natural development outside awareness of intuitive potential that remained imprisoned in psychopathological structures originating in trauma and relational silence.

Even emotional understanding of the past, which at a certain point during analysis becomes possible, testifies to the analysand's empathic receptiveness having widened.

If the function that enables emotions to be understood is unconscious, then it is the task of psychoanalysis to understand what the internal, traumatic, and iatrogenic causes of its malfunction are, and to look for original ways to reach self-awareness.

The unconscious as implicit memory, emotional awareness, and intersubjective and relational experience allows us to catch a glimpse of new worlds where functions of the mind operate outside awareness, and whose immense importance for personality development we are beginning to appreciate.

CHAPTER 6

Non-validation of emotional experience

From what I have written in the previous chapter, it may be inferred that we have a memory laden with meaning but without words.

The 'ineffable' unconscious, not in a mystical but an ungraspable sense, supports us but escapes us, too; it is the implicit emotional memory of each word, including the analysand's, which may not get said, not to conceal or repress, but because perceiving and saying must yet be learnt.

The child's awareness of emotional trauma, caused by the primary object's lack of reciprocity and sharing of experience, remains unexpressed until the patient encounters an experience with an adult equipped with these abilities, such as is found in analysis.

Many patients believe that dreams can sense or see things, but tapping into dreams rarely occurs until someone (the analyst) uses this quality and hands it over to the dreamer; delivering it is not enough, though, because until basic trust in emotional knowledge is once again established, one may continue to 'see' but not 'perceive'.

If a child does not receive emotional validation from his parents, identity perception will not be structured and defects of the self will be produced, as will panic attacks, a sense of inconsistency, and claustrophobic or agoraphobic anxiety. I shall try to illustrate this process in the clinical material that follows.

Perception of emotional reality

Money-Kyrle (1971) believed that since the human psyche has a tendency to alter reality, the purpose of psychoanalysis is to help the patient remove distortions that conceal what he knows innately.

According to this hypothesis, in our unconscious is a potential ability to distinguish between psychic reality and falsifying fantasies; moreover, part of our psyche keeps unconscious perception of the truth intact despite defensive distortion.

However, the passage described by Money-Kyrle is not so linear, as numerous difficulties make transformational work complex. The analysand's perception of his emotional world develops gradually and not without difficulty in the analytic relationship; its manifestation and growth greatly depend on the quality of the original objects, on infantile emotional traumas, and on the patient's pathology (as well as the analyst's receptiveness).

Analysis may be perceived as an exercise of patience by both participants. In his work, the analyst formulates many thoughts that must dwell at length inside him before being communicated to and understood by the patient. And only over time can the analysand develop an ability to perceive an element of psychic truth; at this point, new thoughts can be developed and the falseness of beliefs taken in, beliefs that had propped him up but which he can now let go of since they are no longer of any use. When he allows the field of emotions to enter his inner world, he feels he is 'discovering' a new reality, and this is the experience of growth that makes personality integration and enrichment possible.

I would like to illustrate this initial moment of transformation with clinical material involving a female patient who was brought to me in supervision.

A patient

Carla is thirty or so and is an only child. Just recently, after approximately one year of analysis, she managed to leave her parents' home and go and live with her boyfriend, who makes her feel solid and secure.

In addition to panic attacks, Carla suffers from many anxieties that prevent her from staying on her own. When she gets home from work in the evenings and her boyfriend arrives late, she falls prey to nightmares, she fears for her life, and she sees potential delinquents who are ready to harm her.

Carla's relationship with her parents is unusual. As an only child, she feels very busy supporting them, but her attention towards them mainly derives from her anxiety. She is particularly worried, not only about their physical health, but also their affective relationship. Frequently, she rushes home to check her mother's condition (she suffers from a chronic muscular disease), and that her father is there for his wife when he ought to be.

She derives no pleasure from being close to her parents, and even feels bothered should they suggest she spend some time with them. It seems that in her childhood, Carla did not feel them as living, breathing flesh and blood capable of transmitting *joie de vivre*: perhaps all three of them lived together without really loving each other or enjoying their relationship.

Carla seems younger than she is. Even her posture is childlike, and she looks as though she has no feminine grace, a little automaton always on the move. She is a support worker in a centre for handicapped children, giving the impression that she does her job impulsively, even though she is very interested in her work.

Extremely tied to her analysis, she arrives punctually to her sessions, which recently have become four per week. During a recent session, she said that the previous night she had slept at the centre and had two dreams.

In the first dream, the analyst appears for the first time. Carla is inside a shower cubicle and from behind the glass she vaguely makes out her analyst's figure, cuddling a little girl, perhaps his daughter. Whereas in the dream she thinks that her analyst is a good dad, and is happy about this, she feels angry too at the same time. Then he distances himself from her and Carla heads for a room to fetch her jacket and bag. Here, she sees her analyst with other people, including the little girl from before.

In the second dream, the patient is with Stefano (an instructor at the gym she goes to); they are walking hand in hand or with their arms around each other, talking about lesson times. They are in a beautiful garden, walking along paths abundantly lined with flowers that lead to a wonderful house with a monumental staircase adorned with statues that runs up to the entrance. They both walk up towards the door where they are received by female twins, who look at Carla with an air of rage and wickedness; the house seems full of witchery—it is dark and frightening.

This patient is not very ill and has a good sense of reality, but she is not without complexity. One aspect of this is that despite living with Mario, whom she considers her boyfriend, she is secretly in love with Stefano, the character in the dream, her gym instructor. With him, she entertains the fantasy of a romantic life that takes up part of her day. This aspect was of concern to the analyst; although he considered it as symptomatic of a broader problem, it could not be excluded that this romantic fantasy might involve the analyst in the transference, even though there had yet been no signs of this.

The patient had dreamt about the analyst *for the first time*, and she dreamt about him as a human object in a dimension of separateness. The analyst in the dream had his own life, he was in touch with a daughter of his, and when parting, he also had relations with other people. The patient added that in the dream, once in the room, she was ashamed of being noticed by the analyst and by others present.

I believe that this dream is one of the signs that emotional transformation is occurring. The patient dreamt about the analyst for the first time, perceiving him with ambivalent feelings within an affective relationship, and it is precisely this change that is beginning to occur.

What Carla catches a glimpse of in the dream is the beginning of an emotional relationship (she only catches a glimpse because it seems she still does not have clear vision: she is in a shower cubicle, with an opacifying pane of glass that contains her). In this relationship, human feelings, conflictual by nature, begin to appear: there is pleasure at seeing the analyst who can have emotions, irritation at their being directed towards a child-sister (the patient is an only child), and humiliation from a narcissistic superego that makes her feel full of shame when her emotional state is perceived by others.

If this dream can be considered as the beginning of emotional awareness, what can we say about the second dream, in which Carla sees herself with her arm around Stefano in a Garden of Eden? Why is this marvellous house inaccessible to the two lovers, and dark and threatening for that matter?

The first dream can be seen as the birth of an emotional thought, and the second as a flight into fantasy, a non-thought. Using Bionian terminology, the first dream could be categorised as K and the as second -K.

If we can make a distinction between our imagination that senses our own and others' psychic reality, and our imagination that serves to flee from psychic reality, then we can make the same distinction in relation to dreams. A ridge separates these two positions: *dreaming to intuit* or *dreaming to escape in delirium*.

In a *dream-thought* (dreaming to intuit), the dream is a symbolic transposition of an emotional experience, and in this case, dream images refer to thoughts that seek to integrate the dreamer's emotional life, his defences, and his unconscious fantasies.

In the *dream-escape-delirium*, there is a flight from emotional reality, which gets replaced by another entirely gratifying reality.

A life in fantasy

We know that Carla lives part of her life nurturing a romantic fantasy with her imagination. This is the position that appears in the second dream, where reality is too good to be true, especially when compared to the emotional complexity experienced in the first.

Another important aspect of this dream is that the beautiful house, access to which is via a great staircase, refers to the grandiosity of the fantasy world. Importantly, however, it is inaccessible and fraught with persecution and darkness. The figures of the twins are this, and perhaps they theatrically represent female figures whose hatred towards the patient takes the form of persecution. It might be repudiation by Carla's mother for the narcissistic idyll the patient established with the male figure, her father.

In the dream, the sequence in which the wonderful fantasy turns into a wicked and persecutory nightmare is significant. Carla certainly has wonderful fantasies in everyday life, but also persecutory nightmares.

The patient seems fascinated by a psychic withdrawal where she nurtures romantic fantasy relationships; or, rather, *fantasy has a privileged status* compared to reality for Carla. Flight into fantasy, however, shows signs of no longer being a secret unrepresentable withdrawal, as it is visualised in the dream and communicated to her analyst. Carla admits to him that she does not want a real relationship with Stefano because it would mean having to give up her romantic fantasy world.

At this point, we may hypothesise that, in Carla's case, conditions for the development of unconscious emotional functions were originally deficient.

A depressed mother might have been unable to respond to her little girl's affective wish. In addition, in Carla's case, there was early adultification, a reversal of roles; even now, it is the patient who takes care of her parents. Carla's personality bears infantile and adult aspects. According to this hypothesis, one aspect of her mental suffering is the malfunctioning of the apparatus (the emotional unconscious) that could have let her make contact with the perceptive and emotional part of the self so as to achieve real emotional growth.

The patient thus remained without awareness of her own mental and emotional processes and in childhood she supported herself by falsifying her identity, which was destined to collapse in adulthood (and from here, her panic attacks). At this point in the analysis, it seems as if the emotional block is beginning to yield. The analyst's task now is to help the patient perceive and cope with her emotions, and gradually leave the idealisation of her fantasy refuge.

What is it that actually happens in dream work? Grotstein (1981) contended that when we dream, simultaneously there is a silent spectator that the dream is meant for, an observer who observes the plot, verifies and confirms its truths and messages, and a dreamer who understands the dream.

In patients who have not fully developed unconscious functions serving to understand emotional experience, *the dreamer who understands the dream* is missing. Therefore, even when dreams are clear and explicit, like Carla's, it will initially be the analyst and not the analysand who will give them meaning.

CHAPTER 7

Transference and the analytic relationship

Whereas, in psychoanalytic literature, the transference has received major consideration and has always been described as the driving force of change, the same cannot be said regarding the analytic relationship, which does not have a true conceptualisation and in some respects has not been distinguished from the transference proper. My thought is that the analytic relationship, which should not be interpreted as it belongs to the realm of the implicit, is necessary in order to create dependence that helps development and fosters psychic change.

I shall begin by providing some points on the various transference conceptualisations, particularly those formulated by Freud and Klein, and I shall then outline some of the more recent perspectives that differ greatly from the original ones.

Transference

As we know, Freud was the first to stress the importance of interpreting the transference over the course of the analytic process. His idea was that the patient transferred his infantile complex onto the new figure of the analyst, who therefore came to represent both the parent of the past and a new object: past as well as present were there, operating simultaneously. Interpreting the transference was essential to help the patient differentiate between the present and the inheritance of his childhood past, and to reconstruct the past. Freud considered the transference as the transfer of experiences with past objects onto the person of the analyst. These feelings and perceptions could appear in their original form or be disguised or deformed; the patient's perception of the analyst was influenced by the fact that reactivated mnestic images were integrated into current perceptions, modifying them as a consequence.

Klein broadened the concept of transference by adding projections of parts of the patient into the analyst via splitting and projection. This is why therapeutic work had to involve reintegrating these split-off and projected parts. Klein explained her conception of transference 'in terms of *total situations* transferred from the past into the present, as well as emotions, defences and object relations' (1952, p. 534), and maintained that 'transference originates in the same processes which in the earliest stages determine object-relations' (p. 531).

The term *narcissistic transference*, introduced by Kohut (1971), which he then replaced with 'self–object transference', testifies to the semantic expansion of transference that goes as far as incorporating narcissism. Bezoari (2002) rightly points out that Freud placed the two terms 'transference' and 'narcissism' in opposition to one another.

Bion (1965) defined those features of the transference that originate in repression and concern neurotic patients in particular as '*rigid motion transformations*', and those features produced in the transference by projective identification, common to psychotic patients, as '*projective transformations*'.

A much-debated topic in the past was the illusory nature of the transference. Taking up the concept of the 'false connection' that Freud had initially applied to the transference, some analysts such as Greenson (1965) outlined the distortion produced in the transference regarding the real figure of the analyst. A dichotomy thus becomes endorsed between the transference, in which the patient has a distorted perception of the analyst, and the 'real relationship', in which he is able to maintain a relationship with the real analyst, where perception can be freed of transference distortions. This double vision, illusional and real, allows interpretation work to take the patient back to the past and distinguish it from the present.

The analyst's neutral attitude, allowing the transference to form, remains just a notion. It is not in fact possible that the patient will not pick up on real aspects of the analyst's personality that end up in the transference. This can be taken to the extreme when the analyst unconsciously becomes mixed up with the past traumatic object because of his prolonged lack of emotional receptiveness, an occurrence that is a harbinger of an *analytic impasse.*

In some recent models, the transference has lost its significance as a structural link to the past, and its interpretation is no longer fundamental in clinical work. An example of its refoundation can be found in Fosshage's (1994) thinking, where, not unlike intersubjective authors, he has put forward a model of the transference as 'organisation' in opposition to the transference as 'displacement'. The transference here corresponds to 'primary organising patterns' the analysand uses to construct and assimilate his experience of the analytic relationship. These patterns, as Fosshage underlines, are *activated*, not *transferred*, and consequently it is more appropriate to speak of *organising activity* than *transference.*

For other intersubjective authors, too, the transference is the way in which the experience with the analyst is structured according to an unconscious organising principle. The mind is born into and develops within an intersubjective context, where deeply unconscious preverbal and pre-reflective self–other relationship patterns are formed that serve to organise subsequent experience. The transference thus sheds light on the quality of organising principles. According to intersubjective authors, a neutral analyst cannot exist in that he too takes part in the formation of the transference through his own unconscious organising principles.

In my opinion, this way of seeing means there is no longer a distinction between transference and the analytic relationship.

The analytic relationship

The analytic relationship is connected to the Freudian notion of the 'unobjectionable' positive transference that coexists with strictly projective forms. Freud's unobjectionable transference was a first attempt at theorising the area of the analytic relationship, distinguishing it from the transference proper.

The analytic relationship depends on the analytic function of the analyst's mind, resulting in the formation of a specific relationship with the patient. The distinction between the analyst as a real person and the transference distortion is not relevant here, Greenson having raised issues in this regard.

With his intuitive perception, the patient grasps several aspects of the analyst's functioning and often reproduces them in dreams or associations. This means that, despite his suffering, the patient maintains an acute perception of the analyst's intuitive ability and analytic skill in relation to his conscious and unconscious communications. Of the two terms that make up *analytic relationship*, the first in particular must be borne in mind, as it is the analysing function of the analyst's mind that establishes the relationship. The patient 'unconsciously knows' what his 'nourishment' should be, and he expects it to be administered in terms of thoughts that will broaden his horizons and stimulate his ability to think.

When analytic competence fails, the patient registers what has happened and the analytic relationship can become strained. Perception of the failure or distortion of the analytic response is unconsciously registered, and, in many cases, it is repressed to avoid a conflict or a feeling of guilt. Only when the analyst's receptiveness fails repeatedly and the patient's effort to indicate this runs out is an impasse produced.

The analytic relationship begins to form from the very start: as the patient talks about his life and its events, he takes note of how the analyst does or does not respond. Something similar to what happens during the process of attachment occurs: the child stirs and structures a bond according to the responses he receives from his caregiver, and once formed, this bond will be the base of his security. If we take it that the transference forms from the first words that are exchanged, then the same can be said regarding the analytic relationship. At times, after the first encounters between an analyst and a patient, a sticking point in the initial analytic relationship can result in an end to the process.

In addition to the transference, the therapist must also, and above all, rely on the analytic relationship when treating his patients. Correct interpretation of the transference is of utmost importance, given that this is what reinforces the analytic relationship, ridding it of the past and the patient's projections. Moreover, the value of the interpretation is understood by the patient, as it puts him in contact with psychic truth. Consequently, he gains more trust in the therapy.

The transformational object

It is therefore important to distinguish the transference and countertransference from the analytic relationship. Simply put, the transference is predominantly the work of the patient's projections, his split-off parts, and his childhood past, whereas the analytic relationship is a new construction, resulting from the encounter between the analysand's and the analyst's receptive parts, both parties contributing to its development.

The analytic relationship depends on the analyst's ability to create and keep a place (Di Chiara, 1985) in his mind for the patient, an individual with his own story, his emotional difficulties, his implicit request for mental growth, and his readiness to consider the analyst as a *transformational object* (Bollas, 1979), that is, an object needed for development. As long as this basic bond is kept alive, the analytic process will move forward.

As I have mentioned, the transference, the countertransference, and the analytic relationship are processes that coexist and influence one another reciprocally. Although the transference involves the patient's projections and his past, it also depends on the analyst's conscious and unconscious responses. For example, a negative transference, which may remind the patient of the way he reacted to his father in childhood, could be encouraged by an attitude on the analyst's part that lacks empathy. In other words, the analytic relationship is based on a natural need to depend on an object for one's mental growth, and the nature of that relationship will depend on the analyst's receptiveness and his ability to respond emotionally to the patient's communications.

The analytic relationship is directed towards the future. It is the space where totally new emotional experiences requiring participation and sharing take shape for deprived or traumatised patients. The traumatic experience's concrete nature halted the development of the patient's potential space, and until a new object and a new experience are present in his inner world, this halt is destined to last.

CHAPTER 8

Impasse

Today, satisfactory and attuned emotional responses by the caregiver are thought to be fundamental to a child's development, a change of perspective that is also reflected in clinical work.

Until approximately twenty years ago, much analytic literature concerned itself with the *negative therapeutic reaction*, or rather that event which leads to a halt in the therapeutic process. The original hypothesis put forward by Freud was that this arrest derived from the patient's unconscious negative forces in order to maintain his illness, the patient gaining secondary advantages in the process.

Today, the term *negative therapeutic reaction* has disappeared from psychoanalytic vocabulary, a more neutral and less blaming term, *analytic impasse*, having replaced it. If an impasse should occur after a period of relative progress in the analytic process, it is likely to depend on the analyst's lack of receptiveness to the patient's communications and not on the patient's attempt to boycott the analysis. Over recent decades, reflection on the analytic impasse has gone hand in hand with greater attention to the countertransference, that is, to the analyst's feelings towards the patient.

During the first stage of the analysis, the analyst may have been a helpful object to the analysand's development, but perhaps then less able to support him in his attempts to reach greater levels of independence and competence. The analyst may have found himself in the same condition as a mother who is able to be in good contact with her young child, but unable to manage his adolescence or his journey of independence from the family environment. In this case, the process of development stops because the figure of the analyst unconsciously comes to coincide with the original object, with his qualities but also his limits: he is unable to be a new object (Brenman, 2006). An impasse is evidence that the analytic relationship has deteriorated or is jammed.

The concept of the analytic impasse is a recent one, deriving from the vision of therapy as a process of development with its story and natural evolution.

The psychoanalytic process is a close relationship between two people and not so much a patient resisting his analyst's therapy. Herbert Rosenfeld (1987) defined with extreme clarity the concept of impasse as an interruption to the patient's communication and projective identifications towards the analyst. He described the second analysis of a patient who felt she had failed during her previous therapy; over the course of this second therapy, it became clear that what had actually happened was an impasse, which then became possible to resolve.

Transference psychosis as an impasse

At times, a definitive impasse may not occur but microfractures in analytic communication might. We can often understand via the patient's responses or non-responses whether a certain kind of interpretation created a misunderstanding in the analytic relationship. In such a case, it is necessary to talk to the patient about what happened in order to get the analytic process up and running again.

In an earlier work of mine (2006), I described a borderline patient who, after my repeated interpretative blindness, developed a transference psychosis with a delusion involving me in which I was equated with his psychotic mother. Reflecting on and discussing with the patient my wrong interpretations allowed the psychoanalytic process to start up again.

At times, the halt does not depend on the analyst's receptive distortions but on the patient's anxieties in relation to possible change, which in turn can block analytic development. Distinguishing between these two conditions is essential.

If an analyst finds himself in this kind of situation, what happened needs to be carefully considered, even with the help of colleagues. A particular form of impasse can develop in the analytic treatment of severe borderline patients or those with marked psychotic aspects. In this case, the impasse manifests with a delusional form in which the analyst takes on the character of a persecutor, as happened in the case I have just mentioned. Peculiarly, the patient does not have a generalised delusion that also includes external reality, the persecution and reality distortion concerns solely the figure of the analyst. This situation is referred to as transference psychosis, which must be set apart from psychotic or delusional transference proper, in which the analyst is included in a pre-existing delusion. Transference psychosis is an analytic impasse experienced on a delusional front. In all probability, the analyst will have given interpretations that were either wrong or out of context, but likely negative, and for the patient, he then becomes a true persecutor. Even in this case, the impasse can be overcome if the analyst realises what has happened and tries, with the patient's help, to find the reasons why he was transformed into a persecutor.

Impasse in dreams

Some patients who are more sensitive than others to impasse, and very sensitive to the analyst's failed analytic receptiveness, are those whose pathology developed precisely because of their primary objects' failed receptiveness. These patients have doubts regarding their perceptions and they suffer constant inner confusion, which is projected into the analyst, who in turn can increase the confusion with his responses, unless, that is, he understands what is happening.

Patients who experienced early emotional traumas, whose parents were not bad people but unable to understand their child's mental development, have huge potential for development when they come for analysis, despite at times seeming as if they are severe cases. Important here is that the analyst be receptive. An impasse is created when the analyst reproduces the same behaviours as the parents, and, instead of being a new object, he unconsciously behaves like the original object.

These same patients sometimes represent the unconsciously sensed impasse in their dreams, which must then be clarified. The following clinical material demonstrates this theory.

The patient is a twenty-four-year-old woman who came for analysis because of her mother's untimely death. From her story, it emerged that this girl never felt understood by her mother, who systematically evaded her questions. After three years of analysis, it seemed that the same pattern was being reproduced with me. For some time, without knowing why, the patient began to skip her sessions, or arrive very late when she did show up.

At a certain point, she brought a dream: a female friend of hers gave her back four ice-cream bowls; they were dented, however, when returned, which made the patient go into a rage and she ended up totally destroying the bowls. She associated the four bowls with the breast and realised there and then that a past problem with her mother that had always been difficult for her to understand, and which until then she had forgotten about, was becoming clear in her mind.

She remembered how, in childhood, in her relationship with her mother, there had been long periods in which she had felt she was not able to understand or be understood, without ever knowing whether this depended on her or on her mother. It became clear to me at that moment that the four bowls represented the four sessions in which she had given me her communications, and I had returned them in a deformed fashion, which made her so angry that she wouldn't speak.

With this dream, the patient had been able to describe her state of confusion and explain her destructive anger when she felt she had not been understood by interpretations in her session (the bowls). The dream also cast light on a problem from the past, which had blocked her experience and made her confused: it was still active in the present and unconsciously continued to alter the analytic situation.

This clinical example represents a common-enough situation in analytic work. The analytic process comes to a temporary halt, which has no dramatic or disruptive effects. Then the time comes when the patient expresses, in the clarifying and symbolic language of the dream, the nature of his difficulty, and understanding the dream then marks a turning point and the process gets back on track.

CHAPTER 9

Countertransference

The countertransference, that is, our constant attention towards our own feelings in the consulting room, has two functions: it tells us something about the patient's unconscious communication, and at the same time, it lets us know that some of our emotions may interfere with listening to the analysand and lead to a block in the analytic process.

Regarding the importance given to the analyst's subjective participation in the therapeutic process, two tendencies have gained credibility in countertransference theorising: the first envisages a contained use and the second a broad use. The former tendency holds that the analyst's emotional response is useful, above all, to understand what the patient communicates beyond his words: as for the latter, the arguments vary.

For example, Betty Joseph (1985) claimed that most of the patient's communications refer to the analyst, who, being included in the analysand's defence organisation, would be prompted to act rather than interpret unless he used his own countertransference at all times. Ogden, instead, considers the analyst's dream state, reverie, and free associations to be the determining factors of interpretation.

How the concept has evolved

For Freud, the analyst had to remain benevolently neutral in relation to his patient, who could thus project infantile conflicts onto him, and he in turn could then interpret them and make them conscious. It is interesting to note, however, that Freud himself did not follow these indications, as is documented by a lively and intelligent article written by Luciana Nissim Momigliano (1987) titled 'A spell in Vienna—but was Freud a Freudian?' Freud engaged with, discussed with, and even gave advice to his analysands, expressing unfriendliness towards some, but taking to lunch those he found agreeable.

Freud's recommendations to his pupils to be rigorously neutral derived from the need to bestow scientific status upon psychoanalysis, so that it could not be contaminated by subjectivity. Consequently, the countertransference needed to be considered as dysfunctional and deriving from the analyst's incomplete analysis.

Freud certainly had in mind what had happened to Jung, and also Ferenczi, both of whom had left the countertransference unchecked and become involved with their patients.

Ferenczi (1919) then became the first analyst to stress the importance of the countertransference as an instrument that lets the analyst know many things about himself in relation to the patient, who, in turn, can understand how the analyst's personality and conflicts influence his thought processes.

Adolph Stern (1924) distinguished between two kinds of countertransference: one that derived from the analyst's personal conflicts, and which was therefore an obstacle, and another that was the analyst's response to the patient's transference.

After Stern, others such as Deutsch (1955), Glover (1927), and Strachey (1934) did not write specifically on the countertransference itself but concerned themselves mainly with how to formulate the analytic interpretation and consider what its therapeutic value was.

Later, the countertransference obtained full recognition with Paula Heimann's (1950) work, which turned Freud's assumption of analytic neutrality completely on its head. Her theory was that the analyst's emotional response to the patient was one of the most important research tools with which to understand the patient's unconscious.

With Heimann, the analyst's emotional participation became a necessary therapeutic tool. Countertransference was the patient's creation, an expression of a part of his personality that the analyst emotionally reacted to. Heimann gave as a clinical example a patient who, at the very start of his analysis, said that he wanted to marry a woman he had just met. Heimann reacted worriedly, especially when the patient mentioned his partner's mental condition. Following this, a dream made it possible to understand that her patient's wish could be equated with a sadomasochistic disposition that drove him to falsely act out maturity in the transference. Paula Heimann underlined that in this case the countertransference (the perception of feeling perturbed) served as a criterion to formulate a selective interpretation from material that lent itself to multiple meanings. As a determining factor, she chose her worry in relation to the patient, who wanted to show the analyst that he had reached an adult condition in order to flee from analytic dependence that he was experiencing as humiliating.

We know that Klein did not appreciate Heimann's work, which was in fact one of the reasons why their long-standing friendship ended. Klein's viewpoint on countertransference did not diverge much from Freud's, that is, it was the analyst's pathological expression. In fact, she saw it as an unwelcome emotional response by an analyst who was too involved, too dominated by, or in opposition to the patient. In a seminar held in 1958, she said: 'I have never found that the countertransference has helped me to understand my patient better. If I may put it like this, I have found that it helped me to understand myself better' (Spillius, 2007, p. 78). And she added, 'Where countertransference is unavoidable, it should be controlled, studied and used by the analyst for his own benefit, I would say, and not for the benefit of the patient, I don't believe in it' (Spillius, 2007, p. 79).

It is interesting to note that even though Klein (1946) was the first to have described the mechanism of projective identification, she did not use it in this case to understand and broaden the meaning of the countertransference.

Worth noting is Betty Joseph's (1985) well-known article 'Transference: the total situation', in which this author developed the idea that the transference permeates every communication between analyst and patient. Both are engaged in a total relationship to the extent that it is right to ask oneself whether it is helpful to interpret the transference and the countertransference also in relation to the past, and Joseph believed that it was not necessary to make this kind of connection because it could have upset what was going on in the session.

On the same wavelength is Irma Pick (1985), who stated that the patient's constant projecting into the analyst is the essence of analysis. The patient's projective identifications are like actions that seek to produce reactions in the analyst; interpreting and the very decision to provide an interpretation are not a partial selection of material but a creative act by the analyst.

The unconscious bases of the countertransference

In every analysis, as well as conscious verbal communication, there is also silent unconscious communication.

Freud was the first to have described it in relation to the analyst's unconscious as a receptive organ that allowed him to make contact with the patient's unconscious.

In his paper 'The unconscious' (1915e), Freud noted that a person's unconscious can react to another's, circumventing consciousness.

Authors that underline the importance of the countertransference for the purpose of the analytic process claim that, precisely due to unconscious communication between patient and analyst (and vice versa), the analyst can better understand several important elements for the therapy.

How does this communication between two minds come about?

Money-Kyrle (1956) and later Bion (1967) thought that the analyst functioned as a container that took inside the patient's difficult experiences. Just as a child projects his discomfort and conveys it through crying, and his mother in turn perceives it, the same occurs between patient and analyst.

This viewpoint is based on a gradual reformulation of projective identification by post-Kleinian authors, Bion in particular. Whereas Klein saw projective identification as a psychotic mechanism through which the patient projects parts of his self into the object, resulting in his feeling confused or being persecuted by the object he has projected into, in this subsequent conceptualisation, stress moves away from the patient to the subject who receives the projection, projective identification thus becoming a *communicative projection*.

Given that due to its very nature, projective identification consists of placing parts of the self into the object, the analyst necessarily finds himself at the receiving end of the projections, and if he can become attuned to them, he can therefore understand what is happening. In this sense, projective identification, however it may be motivated, acts as a communication and it is what a positive use for countertransference is based on.

At this point, the countertransference becomes the representation of what the patient consciously or unconsciously projects into the analyst. The latter takes on the role of a receptive organ for the projection and the projective identification.

Racker (1953, 1957) opened up other horizons with his description of different kinds of countertransference: some of the analyst's reactions depend on his identifications with the patient's internal objects and are therefore *complementary* identifications, whereas others are identifications with the analysand's impulses and ego state, and so are *concordant* identifications. For instance, Racker distinguished between direct and indirect countertransference reactions: the former are those that are stimulated by the patient, whereas the latter originate in the environment, in teachers, supervisors, colleagues, or other significant people who influence the analyst. In other conditions, the analyst can be influenced by his own reactions to the analysand's world. A male analyst may develop feelings of rivalry towards the partner of his female patient as a reactivation of the oedipal conflict, for instance.

A contribution by Money-Kyrle (1956) is extremely interesting: when the patient speaks, the analyst identifies with him and, having understood him from inside, he reprojects and in turn interprets. When, however, the analyst does not understand, which happens from time to time, he becomes consciously or unconsciously anxious, his anxiety further inhibits his understanding, and a vicious circle is thus created, which constitutes a deviation from the normal countertransference. The intensity of the analyst's upset, according to Money-Kyrle, depends on the strictness of his superego: if it is protective and friendly, the analyst can tolerate his limits without being excessively troubled, and can regain contact with the patient more easily; if, however, it is very strict, the analyst can develop a depressive or persecutory sense of guilt. As a defence against these unbearable feelings, he can begin to reprimand the patient and feel angry towards him. Money-Kyrle's work shows us how the analyst's undigested emotions tend to be re-projected into the patient with the effect of producing an impasse in the analytic process. Only a careful analysis of the countertransference by the analyst can re-establish the conditions that are necessary in order to continue the analytic process.

Countertransference as reverie

Some contemporary analysts have extended the analyst's subjective contribution to interpretation formulation considerably, thus broadening the field of the countertransference.

I would like to briefly mention a group of colleagues (e.g., Ogden, Grotstein, and Ferro) who refer to Bion's thought in their work.

Reading them, one cannot avoid the impression that their imaginative ability overrides adherence to the clinical data. It is well-known that Bion spoke of reverie to refer to the mother's ability to sense the child's mental state and see to his wishes and needs. This word has taken on a very broad and somewhat different meaning by these authors in comparison to what Bion had attributed to it. Deriving from *rêve* (let us remember the importance Bion gave to 'dreaming while awake'), the word reverie has gradually come to include, in addition to the analyst's intuition about the patient's communication, other meanings such as daydreaming, fantasy, and the dream state. According to these authors, in order that a significant response may be reached, the analyst needs to use his fantasising ability in relation to a stimulus from the patient.

Ogden (1994) maintains that through a profoundly interactive process, each analyst gives expression to experiences projected by the patient in a way that is totally personal. Consequently, conflicts, dynamics, and even the patient's past are uniquely 'created' by each member of the analytic pair, given that the analytic process implies actualising new intersubjective events that did not exist before in the analyst's or in the analysand's affective life. Coherently, Ogden uses the term countertransference to refer not to an identifiable entity that is constructed in response to the transference, but to an aspect of the intersubjective whole generated by the analytic pair (the analytic third), which is experienced separately and individually by the analyst and the analysand. It is this new object that constitutes the matrix within which meanings in the analytic situation are generated.

Given that the patient is unable to 'dream' his own story and life, his communication serves to let the analyst 'dream' and then return the dream to the patient. Therefore, essential to analysis is the analyst's ability to dream the patient's undreamt dreams.

In Ogden's intersubjective vision, the link to clinical work is fuzzy and distant, and the bedrocks of analytic clinical work, such as the laws of mental development, the relationship between conscious and unconscious, the patient's emotional history, and his psychopathology, tend to lose their meaning.

This model assumes that, from the beginning of the analysis, regardless of the patient's pathological structure and history, there is a continuous exchange between the patient's and the analyst's unconscious. In particular, the analyst's unconscious and his reverie not only function as receptive organs but also as transformational tools, hence the importance of the countertransference, which becomes a part of the intersubjective unit generated by the analytic pair.

What is odd about this development is that these authors refer to Bion, who was very careful about widening the countertransference in clinical practice:

> It is a term which should apply to the unconsciously motivated feeling which the analyst is having about the analysand in the analytic situation. The term should be correctly used, as should all terms used by the psychoanalyst. This is not a pedantic matter; it is dictated by the fact that our chosen tools, as it were, are words. If we use them wrongly we soon find ourselves in the position of a sculptor using a blunt instrument.

Conclusions

A useful consideration is that each patient, starting from his psychopathological structure, can create a typical and, to a certain extent, a predictable countertransference.

If, for example, we take a narcissistic patient, we must expect that for quite some time, the analyst will have to bear pressure from the patient aimed at making him feel inferior and envious of the patient's successes.

Thinking instead of the position that a melancholic patient would assign to an analyst, his feeling of not existing would derive from the patient's propaganda on the uselessness of both the analysis and the analyst. We know how much of an expert the melancholic is at tormenting the object and how he finds paradoxical relief in making his interlocutor depressed, depriving him of any pleasure (in the case of analysis, depriving the analyst of therapeutic satisfaction). Not even here can the analyst throw in the towel, but just keep himself alive and endure one more minute longer than the patient.

But the patient's projections are not always negative. There are cases in which the analyst must resist being seduced, and, in fact, not infrequently do patients seek a privileged bond with the analyst, tickling his narcissism. One of the most common behaviours is the patient trying to convince the analyst of his own version of the facts. The analyst, therefore, needs to continually keep his bearings in a bid to distinguish between what is real and what is distorted by the patient's projections.

One last point concerns the therapeutic value of the countertransference.

I am of the belief that using the countertransference to understand how the patient uses the analyst is not enough to promote therapeutic development; almost total stress placed on it reduces the developmental potential of the analysis, it discourages analytic freedom, and creates a claustrophobic atmosphere. The patient, generally speaking, pays a great deal of attention to how the analyst behaves in the relationship with him. The analytic relationship is formed and sustained also because of the analyst's ability to identify the most meaningful part in what is communicated between him and the patient. This is why the analyst must be free of what Racker defines as *indirect* countertransference reactions, that is, an attitude that is too unilaterally aligned with viewpoints of the predominant analytic culture at a given time in the society the analyst belongs to.

In other words, analysing the countertransference is essential to keep therapeutic potential open, but it does not constitute a therapeutic element in itself. Rather than the countertransference, I consider the exploration of the patient's inner world as more important, along with his traumatic history, especially the presence of intrusive objects that have become part of him and contributed to creating pathological structures proper.

Due to these considerations, I believe that the analyst should not limit himself to understanding only the projections the patient directs at him, but he must also integrate the patient's world, providing all that can be helpful for the patient's psychic development: memories, reconstructions, reflections, life experience, and so forth. This close creative experience will enable the patient to learn from the emotional reality of the relationship and to find his own personal meaning.

Within this perspective, analysing the countertransference cannot but have a moderate and contained use.

CHAPTER 10

Regression

As stated earlier, psychoanalysis is a unitary discipline that contains various explanatory models with different theories of mental development, plus factors that promote it as well as causes that create illness. That the various psychoanalytic theories attribute particular relevance to different factors of mental growth, both constitutional and environmental, means that many theories exist.

Regression lends itself well to illustrating the many different theories with different conceptualisations of the same process that coexist in the corpus of psychoanalysis. Even though this concept is seldom used today, it is useful to consider it, not only because it has been central to analytic theory for a long time, but also because it expresses a hypothesis on the origin of mental illness.

Before Freud, the concept of regression had been formulated by neurologist John Hughlings Jackson (Jackson, 1969), who had theorised a developmental and hierarchical organisation of various brain areas and functions, in which nerve centres were arranged according to their function, from the oldest to the most recent—that is, a tripartite brain.

Jackson thought of development as a path that went from the primitive to the most developed; at birth, the nervous system is already mainly developed regarding automatic functions, and as it grows, it becomes enriched with more complex functions. Jackson's concept of regression implies a return to older functions when pathology affects the more recently developed areas.

The same idea of basic and complex functions permeates Freud's work. One of its cornerstones is that mental illness consists of a return to more primitive levels of functioning. According to Freud, psychosexual stages of development are never completely overcome, but remain present and potentially active in the individual. Over the course of illness, there is regression to a previous stage of development; the more severe the illness, the more primitive the fixation point.

The 'pathological' thus comes to coincide with the 'primitive'. Abraham, too, who used this idea systematically, sought to classify the various mental disorders according to stages of libidinal development. Melancholy, for instance, had its fixation point in the oral stage, obsessional neurosis in the anal-sadistic stage, whereas hysteria had its fixation in the phallic stage.

For Freud, regression could be considered in a *topical* sense as the inversion of excitation direction along the psychic systems; in a *temporal* sense as the inversion of genetic stages of libidinal development; and in a *formal* sense as a re-actualisation of more primitive behaviours and modes of expression.

Topical regression manifests particularly during sleep. The dream represents primitive psychic functioning that remains throughout adult life: the dreamer regresses to an original psychic system (wishful thinking), in which images take the place of thought. In this case, there is functional regression that allows unconscious wishes, normally kept hidden via repression, to become manifest.

Many phenomena that from the secondary process go back to the primary process can be attributed to *formal regression*, a concept that Freud concerned himself less with. As for *temporal regression*, Freud identified regression that regarded the object, regression that regarded the libidinal stage, and regression that concerned ego development. The concept of regression does not imply the disappearance of the more developed functions but a loss of their supremacy in overall mental functioning for a greater or lesser length of time. As an integral part of it, every mental illness contains a certain degree of regression, which, at the same time, activates the analytic situation, triggering transference development and allowing past experiences to be remembered and relived. The facilitating factor, unique to analytic therapy, is being able to create a favourable climate for childhood-type situations to arise.[1]

Klein did not use the concept of *fixation points* but referred to *position*. In her model, there are no developmental stages connected to body functions (as Freud hypothesised), but ways of relating with objects. There is a more primitive mental functioning mode, the *paranoid–schizoid position*, that contrasts with a more mature one, the *depressive position*. In the paranoid–schizoid position, the frustrating object is hated and attacked in phantasy, and it consequently becomes persecutory; a vicious circle of hate and fear is thus created. In this position, good and bad exist entirely separately; the good object (the good breast and the subject) is idealised, and the bad object (the frustrating object) is hated.

According to Klein, when the mother becomes frustrating, she is transformed by the child into a bad object; when, however, she nourishes and protects him, she is experienced as a good object. Only subsequently can the child sense that the frustrating object and the gratifying object are one and the same, at which point he combines the two experiences of love and hate. During this stage, love becomes an egocentric relationship as well as altruistic attention.

Even in Klein's vision, as in Freud's, primitive functioning coincides with pathological functioning; the more the patient uses paranoid–schizoid position mechanisms, the more he risks illness.

At the 'Controversial Discussions' held in London during the Second World War, psychoanalysts from the Kleinian group sought to clarify their theoretical positions. One of the topics discussed was regression, on which Paula Heimann and Susan Isaacs (1952) wrote a paper to clarify their viewpoint and that of Melanie Klein: according to their thesis, the more the individual is primitive, the more his instinctive forces express aggressiveness, and only by stemming original aggressiveness can mental growth and altruistic object relations development occur.

---

[1] An accurate analytic account of the use of regression in Freud's work can be found in an article by Stanley W. Jackson (1969).

An important point in Isaacs and Heimann's paper concerned the death instinct, as regression is closely connected to persecutory anxiety: the more this anxiety is present, the more psychic development is inhibited. In this case, the child remains tied to a stage of primitive fixation in a bid to control his anxiety. Regression is seen by Heimann and Isaacs not so much as going backwards but as a developmental arrest; indeed, if a child is a carrier of extremely violent anxieties and excessive destructive drives, he cannot but remain fixed to a primitive type of functioning.

We could actually state that Isaacs and Heimann's work, which aimed to show how regression was important to the Kleinian model, marked instead its expiration: their thinking is that regression is equivalent to a block in development and not a backward shift.

In Kleinian-inspired psychoanalytic literature, the term regression was phased out, the latest edition of the Kleinian dictionary (Spillius et al., 2011) bears no mention of it at all. The most explicit comment on the term was by Betty Joseph, a renowned psychoanalyst of the group, who, during her American seminar, when replying to a specific question on the matter, said: 'We do not use it at all (*the term regression*)' (Inderbitzin & Levy, 2000).

Regression in the service of development

Outside Kleinian literature, regression maintained its validity for quite some time, and can be found, albeit with differing degrees of emphasis, in two important groups, one inspired by Anna Freud, the other by Winnicott and his followers.

One of the reasons why it lasted is to do with the fact that regression is explanatory in analytic clinical work, in the sense that it is considered useful for development even though not necessary. This viewpoint was summed up nicely by Balint (1968) as 'regression in the service of progress', and by Kris (1952) as 'regression in the service of the ego'. According to Balint (1968), in the analytic situation, regression is both an intrapsychic and an interpersonal phenomenon in that it can have at least two purposes: gratifying a drive or being recognised by an object. In Balint's view, all regressive states are an attempt to return to primary love and traumas that interfered with it.

Many psychoanalysts followed this direction, sustaining that the purpose of therapy was to promote transference regression that bore similarities to infantile neurosis; in other words, over the course of a patient's analysis, in order that he may develop, he needs to experience a childhood-like regressive state.

Other authors, on the contrary, criticise this conception, considering regression as artificial in those analyses where the analyst applies abstinence to a fault; for this reason, regression would not be physiological but in large part iatrogenic.

As Hartmann (1964) perspicaciously recognised, the hypothesis that what occurs in development can be repeated in clinical work carries the risk of falling into 'genetic fallacy'. In fact, it is not easy to distinguish whether a process is in the area of physiological regression, or whether it is more a case of pathological regression.

A more recent critical position is that of Renik (1998), for whom a good analysis certainly does not need the patient to regress; when this happens, it must be analysed, otherwise the therapy can be seriously distorted.

We might ask ourselves whether the patient actually regresses in the consulting room or whether he allows himself more freedom than usual and can therefore express his emotions more clearly and openly. Being aware of one's feelings or one's aggressiveness does not mean regressing. In this sense, the Sandlers (1984) underlined that the analyst needs to allow the patient to express as well as be able to tolerate his perverse, stupid, childish, and even ridiculous parts.

Freud never spoke of regression as having a therapeutic function, seeing it rather as having a defensive or pathogenic purpose; he implicitly maintained, however, that there cannot be an analytic process without necessary regression.

I have cited these various viewpoints on regression to illustrate how the debate on this topic was broad and complex; it came to bear numerous meanings according to the model it was built into, its distinctiveness then gradually waning.

Winnicott and regression

Regression found original development in Winnicott's (1954) conceptualisation, to which I have dedicated the final part of this chapter.

When Winnicott stated that what is developed can coincide with the non-authentic or the pathological, he naturally called into question the well-consolidated notion in psychoanalytic tradition of equating the primitive with the pathological. To grow, Winnicott claimed, some personality distortion is needed in order to adapt to the requests of one's environment. The true self remains hidden and protected by the structures that are built to defend it from environmental pressures. In this case, the primitive identifies with the healthy parts of the personality that remain unknown to the patient himself.

In Winnicott's thinking, regression loses all its negative meaning and instead is in the service of recovering healthy infantile parts that have remained unexpressed. During analysis, only through a journey backwards can these infantile parts be recovered, and one of the tasks of psychoanalytic therapy is this.[2]

Furthermore, Winnicott closely linked regression to dependence, seeing therapeutic regression as a way of reliving unsuccessful original dependence. Good enough 'holding', represented by the analytic setting, allows the patient to restore hope in processing and overcoming the original trauma so that he may find his true self (Abram, 2002).

Winnicott claimed that, following environmental traumas, memories are 'frozen', and the new psychoanalytic environment can bring about a thaw.

Despite Winnicott's attempts to differentiate between regression that can foster development and pathological regression in severe patients, he was unable, in my opinion, to trace a clear line between the two mental conditions.

For example, he considered psychosis as a pathology connected to early environmental failure, but at the same time thought that the psychotic patient's regression during therapy constituted a return that was necessary in order to start up new development. In this sense, psychosis could be treated with a specific therapeutic relationship that was in line with the patient's corresponding regression.

---

[2] As was done by Winnicott, the concept of regression was assigned a particular meaning by Kohut, too, whose thinking moved away from the view that the primitive was equivalent to the pathological. Narcissism, meaning self-idealisation, was seen as a physiological moment in an individual's development. If a child does not receive an empathic response to his original narcissism, structural gaps are created, that is, psychic flaws destined to lead to the development of psychopathology. For therapeutic purposes, Kohut too believed it was important to return to those primitive modes of self-development that were ignored during development.

To better understand how the concept of regression to dependence can give rise to serious misunderstandings, we can look for a moment at matters concerning a female patient in analysis for three years with Masud Khan (1963), Winnicott's most faithful pupil.

This patient came for therapy after an episode of agitated depression, and the first part of her analysis seemed to go as would be expected. After seven months, however, the patient veered towards a maniacal state, with an omnipotent and idealised transference, soon followed by a collapse into depression and death wishes. According to Khan, this was a moment that corresponded to psychoanalytic regression. Dependence on the analyst was total and the patient seemed to completely abandon herself to this state of painful non-existence. During this three-month episode, Khan felt he needed to remain alive and present, but not interfere using interpretations. Despite the holding, the patient ended up swallowing a heap of pills and needed to be admitted to hospital. In the following months, the patient developed an acute paranoid transference with suicidal threats. During this stage, Khan adopted a more analytically active approach, which seemed to improve the situation a little. The patient finished her analysis with a seemingly good outcome.

Khan considered the patient's depressive episode as the moment when therapeutic regression occurred, which, in his opinion, turned out to be useful for the outcome of therapy. It is strange, however, that Khan did not consider this period as an aspect of the manic-depressive psychopathological process the patient was a bearer of.

This case lends itself well to illustrating how stress placed exclusively on therapeutic regression to dependence can hide the fact that some patients really do regress during analytic treatment, in the sense that they present clinical deterioration that can depend on the pathological process itself or on insufficient analytic involvement. In these cases, it is not so much a case of accessing dependence as it is a desperate state of anxiety with an acute need for reassurance and analytic presence.

Conclusions

We can ask ourselves at this point whether the term regression still bears meaning in psychoanalysis.

Originally, the term helped explain why the individual became ill and it involved a genetic hypothesis on the psychic disorder linked to Freud's hypothesis on psychosexual development: psychic illness coincided with a return to primitive stages, primitive being pathological.

Today, this kind of conceptualisation of psychic disorders is no longer sustainable. Since birth, the infant has specific relating skills, and can therefore not be considered as a primitive being. Moreover, it is increasingly clear that when a child grows up in a quite positive environment, he develops normally, whereas when there are constant emotional traumas or affective deficits, development is inhibited, or worse still, a psychopathological path ensues.

Illness derives from predominantly psychopathological (not physiological) modes of functioning since childhood that progressively gain the upper hand in adulthood.

If we agree with this second hypothesis, we can depart from the concept of regression. Becoming mentally ill depends on psychopathological structures that were created during early development and gradually become part of the individual himself.

CHAPTER 11

Anxiety

Anxiety is a complex concept, since it is brought about by numerous factors and, because of its nature, it is difficult to classify. I shall try to describe it, beginning with its historical evolution.

Let us begin with Freud. In his first model, in which pleasure is the individual's primary goal, anxiety originates if the libidinal drive encounters obstacles when discharged, as it cannot reach its object; in other words, anxiety is the consequence of a libidinal obstruction or a break in narcissistic equilibrium.

For some time, Freud considered this first theory as valid and, even when he considered anxiety as a consequence of trauma, he underlined that the determining factor triggering it was a break in narcissistic equilibrium produced by the trauma.

What, then, are the inner obstacles that prevent pleasure from being achieved? The principal cause is connected to psychic conflict that can arise on the way to feeling pleasure, when mental representations of libidinal wishes are incompatible with consciousness. Anxiety would therefore be the result of psychic work that leads to the repression of wishes. Consistent with this hypothesis, anxiety is not considered as primary, and neither did it become so after the introduction of the dual-drive theory, which would have made it possible to derive anxiety from the death instinct.

From the very beginning, however, Freud described other forms of anxiety, too. In 1895, he wrote 'On the grounds for detaching a particular syndrome from neurasthenia under the description anxiety neurosis' (1895b), where two forms of anxiety are highlighted: in the first, which is psychological proper, the wish is repressed and converted into a symptom; in the second, anxiety is free. In other words, Freud intuited that alongside anxiety caused by psychic dynamics, another non-psychologised form exists that does not originate in emotions or conflicts.

Freud therefore distinguished between 'psychoneuroses', in which anxiety is connected to unconscious conflict content that becomes converted into a somatic symptom, and 'actual neuroses' (phobia or panic), characterised by substantial neurovegetative symptoms, where there is no repression or anxiety transformation.

These neuroses do not therefore derive from psychological factors but are connected to simple physiopathological problems, such as an accumulation of sexual desire that cannot be discharged, according to the well-known hydraulic concept of the libido.

Although some psychoanalysts consider this early intuition of Freud's on the actual neuroses as pre-psychoanalytic, in that it preceded the discovery of the dynamic unconscious, the Oedipus complex, and infantile sexuality, I think that he sensed an important feature of the kind of anxiety that is unleashed in panic attacks, which places it outside the dynamics of conflict. I shall return to this further ahead.

In the economic model just described, anxiety is something that always derives from inside, and its unleashing depends on the external event only secondarily. The external trauma is pathogenic when it encounters an internal complex or it strikes narcissistic equilibrium. This became evident when Freud underlined the role of infantile sexuality and the Oedipus complex.

In the case of 'Little Hans' (1909b), the horse phobia is explained by castration anxiety in relation to the oedipal conflict, whereas in Freud's 'Wolf Man' (1918b), castration anxiety resulting from homosexual desire for the father is the source of the wolf phobia.

It is internal conflict patterns, oedipal in this case, that trigger anxiety originating in defensive action (repression), whose function is to safeguard that part of the personality that wants to be protected from all that is distressful. For Freud, distress was inner excitation, mental representations of that excitation or situations that can arouse it.

To understand Freud's concept of defence, the *idea of conflict* is central, without which there would be no defence, no neurotic disorder, and no anxiety. The conflict derives from two opposing forces in the individual. For Freud, man is fundamentally conflictual because he must appease opposites and serve two masters, the ego and the id. The defence originates in the irreconcilability between an unconscious representation and the ego, and it is called upon to defend the ego from possible distress; in so doing, however, the defence ends up disturbing the ego by producing anxiety. This economic model of anxiety was never abandoned by Freud.

In Freud's later writings, such as *Civilization and its Discontents* (1930a), he presented an ineliminable conflict between nature and culture; civilisation is the stepmother of instinctual life, which, being unable to fully express itself due to the restraints and limits imposed upon it, marks its sacrifice through man's unhappiness and anxiety.

Yet another important contribution was the introduction of the *protective shield* (Freud, 1920g), according to which the mind has a threshold of tolerance for external stimuli, beyond which trauma is produced.

For Freud, it is as if the mind were surrounded by a sort of protective skin that can be perforated or lacerated; when trauma destroys this protective filter, external situations, which can no longer be assimilated selectively, create an overflow of excitation.

With the structural hypothesis in *The Ego and the Id* (1923b) having gained ground, and with the distinction between the three psychic agencies (ego, superego, id), the energy-libido concept was integrated into a new model in which anxiety was no longer seen only as a consequence of an overload of stimuli or as the repression of wish drives: the ego increasingly took on the role of receiver and producer of danger signals, and anxiety derived from conflicts between the various agencies of the personality, for instance, the superego's excessive strictness in relation to the ego.

In *Inhibitions, Symptoms and Anxiety* (1926d), the conceptualisation of anxiety was further enriched; here, Freud stated that anxiety can be a primary fact that does not derive from repression, but, conversely, it can promote repression (and not vice versa).

Anxiety is described as a real danger (*automatic anxiety*) and as a possible danger (*signal anxiety*): the former is triggered by a sudden trauma, whereas signal anxiety warns of a potential inner or outer danger. The five most common dangers that activate signal anxiety are: birth, castration dread, loss of the love object, loss of object love, and annihilation anxiety.

Melanie Klein

Let us now look at Melanie Klein's theory. Beginning with *signal anxiety*, Klein claimed that from birth the ego can receive anxiety that signals danger. The child feels threatened by the death drive that manifests as annihilation or fragmentation anxiety. When death anxiety is projected outwards, it is felt as a danger of being attacked by persecutory entities. Therefore, from the start, a child has to organise defences for his survival, his struggle against anxiety, and his fear of disintegrating or being killed; in order to do this, he must split the object into good and bad, an operation that contributes to an initial structuring of the mind.

Whereas, for Freud, defences against the drive go into action relatively late, when the child must relate to an object of desire (during the oedipal conflict, for instance), for Klein, defences come into action very early on, as they are called upon to protect the child from primary annihilation anxiety.

As we have seen, anxiety is not primary for Freud, instead it derives from drive conflict, and the defence does not act against anxiety but the drive. For Klein, the defence is directed against anxiety, and it even assumes a structuring role in the individual's development.

The first good internal object, that is, maternal care, plays a core role in structuring the ego and favours personality cohesion and integration.

Anxiety in the inner world can be of various types: paranoid–schizoid anxiety, the most primitive, when fear concerns a threat to the self by persecutors; or depressive anxiety, which is more evolved and concerns the love object that is threatened by aggressive phantasies. For Klein (1948), these two types of anxiety are the prototype for all other anxiety. Inevitable fragmentation, solitude, and abandonment anxiety experienced at the beginning of life tends to cyclically reappear throughout our existence. In adult life, this may manifest either as an attack by hostile internal objects or as depressive anxiety when good objects are perceived as threatened by bad internal figures. At any rate, the strength of the ego is directly correlated to an ability to tolerate anxiety, which is what is essential for mental growth.

Klein saw anxiety, together with defences to cope with it, as constituting the crux of psychic development, and she even went on to state that a sufficient amount of anxiety was needed for symbol formation and fantasy development.

One difference between Klein and Freud is their clinical use of the concept of the death instinct. Freud (1920g) did not use it in clinical theory, whereas Klein made it the cornerstone of her understanding of patients' psychopathological manifestations.

Whereas, for Freud, the death instinct is a biological impulse at work inside the organism and of which there is no representation in the unconscious, for Klein, the death instinct, which is present right from our earliest unconscious phantasies, is the basis of anxiety and primitive defence construction.

Still today, Freud's and Klein's contributions on anxiety constitute one of the pillars of psychoanalytic theoretical thought and clinical work. The two positions, which contrast but often integrate with one another, enable a better understanding of theory development and its application to technique.

Freud seemed to underline that anxiety and mental suffering derive from sacrifices imposed by society (parents and the superego) via the repression of the individual's wishes. Klein, however, believed that pain, separation, and mourning are original to the human condition and the newborn's impotence. Both authors paved the way for an extraordinarily innovative conception of mental suffering, which can have various origins: it can originate in man's love wish potential being inhibited, as Freud seemed to suggest, or in areas of suffering connected to conflict between love and destructiveness, as Klein proposed.

Further developments

Let us now consider contributions by subsequent authors. Rather than drive characteristics, some of these took into consideration relational matters that were distorted, lacking, or unsuccessful, thus referring to a child who is not isolated but in relation with his surrounding environment from the very start, his mother in particular.

Winnicott (1965) acutely developed Freud's concept of the protective shield, stating that for newborns and infants, this function is performed by the mother via her intuitive ability.

For Winnicott, the mother is an *adaptive* mother, endowed with an intuitive mind that can instinctively understand her child's needs and anxieties and respond adequately to his level of development.

Alongside *pathological* projective identification, Bion (1965) also described *normal* projective identification *for the purposes of communication*, which functions as a means of communication for emotions not conveyed via verbal channels. He underlined that, for survival, human beings need an object that can take in their emotions. A container is needed that can keep inside the emotional load the child cannot bear. Similar to what happens in analysis, when the analyst receives the patient's silent emotional communication while listening to the countertransference, a mother, through her empathic receptiveness, decodes the child's emotional state and receives his anxiety. For Bion, anxiety is a natural and primitive form of communication that is transmitted to the mother so she can then return it in a bearable form. If a mother cannot carry out this transformation, anxiety then becomes nameless dread.

Meltzer (1966), in reference to those patients with an unbearable level of anxiety, said that they had been unable to make use of the maternal function, which he called toilet-breast, that is, an initial (mental) place where anxiety can be flushed to. If this primitive evacuation is prevented, the child cannot move on to the next stage, which would allow him to become aware of the existence of an 'other' psychic object that can give meaning to his emotions. The mother's empathic receptive function is therefore of utmost importance in accommodating and processing anxiety.

An original vision is John Bowlby's (1980) attachment theory, in which the child's caregiver contributes to developing and modulating his emotional experiences, including anxiety. Bowlby claimed that human beings are motivated by a universal need to create affective bonds. Being able to activate secure attachment behaviour depends on the child having experienced constant patterns of environmental signals. Experiencing security is the goal of the attachment system, which is the regulator par excellence of emotional experience. Regulating affects is not innate but develops when the child experiences a kind of relationship in which his constantly changing signals within his emotional state are understood and receive an adequate response. Many authors (Ainsworth et al., 1978, for instance) have demonstrated with observational data that a child's anxiety containment is achieved through the mother's transmission and mirroring approach.

That the child's caregiver is able to modulate anxiety represents one of the cornerstones of attachment theory and modern psychoanalytic concepts. Starting in infancy and continuing throughout life, mental health is determined by our relationships with attachment figures who provide emotional support and protection from anxiety. A mother's way of dealing with the world and her child's protection requests is fundamental to the development of the child's ability to contain anxiety.

As Bordi (2004) reminded us, attachment theory, following different routes, came to conclusions that are analogous to Bion's, providing, moreover, considerable empirical content. Based on these contributions, we may assume that anxiety takes on a catastrophic meaning in individuals who are unequipped with a symbolic bulwark that can contain physiological imbalance, since adequate maternal mirroring in infancy was not experienced.

During the analytic process, the psychoanalyst carries out the function of an object that can cope with anxiety the patient finds unbearable; the same regulatory strategy as in the first years of life is thus reproduced via the introjection of an internal presence that can sense stress, contain it, and allow it to be mentalized.

What, however, might other events be that prevent this function from being acquired?

Through the concept of cumulative trauma, Khan (1963) describes the effects of prolonged psychic damage in the context of a child's dependence when the mother systematically fails in her function as a protective shield and an auxiliary ego. The mother, thus, does not permit a strategy of sufficient anxiety regulation and mentalization, and she herself becomes an anxiety source. Recent studies, inspired also by neuroscientific data, show that early repeated trauma is incorporated into unconscious memory (procedural) and expressed via automatic responses that perpetuate anxiety. An excess of traumatic anxiety prevents learning, interferes with memory, and opposes the growth and development of relationships.

Traumatic anxiety

When a sudden, destructive event occurs, the catastrophe strikes the individual's sense of self and leaves profound devastation that prevents processing.

As I mentioned earlier, Freud distinguished between anxiety felt as a *real danger* (automatic anxiety) and anxiety felt in the event of *possible danger* (signal anxiety). An anxiety signal alerts the individual to an imminent danger and prepares him for the event: unfortunately, after a traumatic event, the ego is no longer able to distinguish between an anxiety signal and automatic anxiety.

Recent psychoanalytic studies (Davies, 2001), confirmed by neuroscientific discoveries (LeDoux, 1996), tell us that traumatic memories are encoded in the brain differently from standard memories. *Dissociation*, which is the main defence mechanism in these cases, is a radical process that separates thoughts, feelings, memories, and perceptions of the traumatic experiences from the rest of the psyche, enabling the victim to function *as if* the trauma had not happened. Dissociation is 'the escape when there is no escape' (Putnam, 1997).

This defence, which is necessary for mental survival at the time of the trauma, impoverishes the subject and over time produces alterations to psychic processes, compromising the individual's sense of integrity and continuity of existence. Inhibiting both the perception of what happened and access to the memory, dissociation also prevents the trauma from being processed.

When working psychoanalytically with a traumatised person, we can see first-hand how the traumatic event exposed the patient to a concrete experience of death, suddenly placing him before 'nameless dread', and arousing that fear of annihilation that can destructure the mind biologically, even before it is capable of doing so psychologically. The catastrophe that struck a blow to the sense of self leaves deep devastation which prevents the traumatic event from being processed.

For years, if not decades, or the rest of one's life, survivors are unable to return to the places where they were helpless victims of cruelty, where they were worn down by atrocious crimes, or where they were impotent in the face of an event that devastated an emotionally meaningful place or killed loved ones.

I would like to add that given this destabilising effect, the trauma is necessarily experienced in complete solitude and impotence. Subsequent difficulty related to processing the trauma and simultaneous panic anxiety is connected to flashbacks, that is, sudden invasive feelings not of remembering the event but of reliving it in the present. Normally, we can remember an event without reliving it, no matter how vivid it is. Following the destructuring action of trauma, however, the distinction between *the ego* and *the event* is lost, and the individual, who cannot keep the necessary distance from it, is overwhelmed by nameless dread. Remembering the event or thinking back over it in one's mind are no longer possible as they have been replaced by reliving it.

Clinical work

With the aim of distinguishing between some of the more typical anxiety patterns, I would now like to present them according to how they emerge in the clinical context.

First of all, anxiety needs to be thought of as a ubiquitous phenomenon no human activity can escape from. From a certain point of view, anxiety can also be thought of as a danger signal in the service of the healthy part of the personality. As such, it is an important feeling that signals moments of developmental crises, for instance, passing from one stage of our life cycle to another.

A typical situation of this sort is the anxiety crisis in middle age, a time in which the limit of an individual's existence can no longer be denied. Despite having had reasonable psychic balance and a successful life, some people during this period start to feel uneasy, anxious, or depressed. Anxiety in these cases testifies to the fact that those defences (a desire for success, pleasure from a romantic relationship, having a family, or building a career) which contributed to supporting the individual can no longer help him cope with the second part of his life. Extremely acute anxiety can also appear in reactions to abandonment when separation from an affective object is experienced as a collapse of the self. In all these cases, an incapacity to bear psychic pain creates anxiety.

A particular form of anxiety, with paroxysmal tendencies and considerable neurovegetative reactions, is the panic attack, in which the body speaks of its own death, or, rather, its agony. In the panic attack, anxiety is not, however, the sole symptom: a psychosomatic procession accompanies the situation of terror, which is why the attack unleashes a true fear of death.

In clinical work, it is of utmost importance to identify the nature of the conflict that generates the anxiety so that it can be modified. One of the most frequent patterns that maintains the anxiety is an excessively strict, aggressive, and persecutory superego in the patient's inner world.

Both Freud and Klein showed how some forms of psychic suffering are sustained by a primitive superego. An extreme case is melancholy, when the superego becomes a destructive organisation, 'a pure culture of the death instinct' (Freud, 1923b). Such a superego generates instability and anxiety because it is an object that constantly accuses the patient of and reprimands him for inadequacies, generating insecurity and worthlessness. In clinical work, when we treat depressed, narcissistic, or borderline subjects, we are used to observing an excess of death anxiety, expressed via hypochondriacal or persecutory terrors.

In other pathological situations, anxiety is denied, so the alarm signal fails, and its communicative function of a request for help therefore fails, too. In anorexia, for example, the patient has no idea that she is suffering or is ill, and she denies that the prolongation of her anorexic state can lead to death; for the anorexic sufferer, refusing food is more of an extraordinary experience than an abnormal fact. Given the denial, the patient is unaware that her attraction towards this mental state is equivalent to an attraction towards death.

It appears that in some patients, mental areas fraught with self-destructiveness are formed, that is, silent psychotic islands that remain inside the personality, ready to explode should a crisis arise. By idealising destructiveness, anxiety is silenced and replaced by excitement. Something similar happens in the perversions: as opposed to arousing anxiety, wickedness, and cruelty instead stimulate pleasure. In all these cases, idealising destructiveness wipes out anxiety and replaces it with excitement.

CHAPTER 12

Phobia and panic

In this particular period, panic attacks are one of the most widespread psychopathological manifestations, very much like hysteria at the time when psychoanalysis got its start.

This psychopathology is characterised by a sudden and unpredictable onset of episodes of such intense anxiety that they leave an extreme sense of fatigue.

Usually, a panic attack, which is always psychosomatically expressed, is accompanied by strong neurovegetative manifestations such as palpitations, tachycardia, dizziness, tremors, abdominal cramps, widespread or localised pain, hyperidrosis and, above all, a feeling of suffocation. Phobia, however, unlike a panic attack, is not correlated to neurovegetative manifestations, but is active in relation to the threat of the phobic object.

Panic attacks concern first and foremost the body. This narration from *An Armenian Sketchbook* by Vassilj Grossman (2013) paints an acute picture:

> At this point I realised that I was dying. My chest and shoulders were covered in sweat. My heart seemed to be beating separately

> from me … I was overcome by mortal anguish. The horror of dying, of the end of life, grew from second to second. There was a terrible sense of lightness about my body—except that it was no longer my body, my only true home, the home of my 'I'. My body seemed to be forsaking me, abandoning me. Hands, feet, lungs, heart—all were leaving me … And this incorporeal world—this incorporeal universe that had been my 'I'—this was perishing because my fingers, my skull and the muscles of my heart were peeling away from me, slipping out from my 'I' … I was dying, and I was slow to take in that my fingers had once again become my fingers, that I was once again inside them, that my heart was there inside me again and I inside it, that my 'I' was back inside my lungs again, and that my lungs were now breathing oxygen.

Psychoanalysis has shown an interest in panic disorder since the very beginning, with Freud's (1894a, 1895c) pioneering works. Today, however, psychoanalytic contributions that concern themselves specifically with this topic are not many, especially in comparison to the numerous psychiatric, psychopharmacological, and cognitive-behavioural psychology studies.

One reason related to a lack of interest among psychoanalysts for panic attacks may be due to the fact that our discipline does not deal with transforming one single symptom, something that other methods deem possible. For psychoanalysis, there are no stable symptomatic improvements without an overall transformation of the whole personality.

Issues concerning the nature of the panic attack, if it is psychological or physical, greatly influence the choice of therapeutic intervention. I am of the belief that a panic attack has psychic origins that manifest according to a specific automatic neurobiological response. Two moments of the attack can be isolated: one that sees anxiety felt psychically, and the other where body participation prevails, and terror becomes uncontrolled somatic anxiety.

When an individual suffers a panic attack, he is convinced he is going to die; it is his body that talks about death, or, rather, about agony. Psychosomatic symptoms are in the foreground: the mind registers them and translates them into unmistakable messages of an inevitable and definitive catastrophe.

Because of anxiety, breathing and heart rates increase, as does sweating, and panic dilates, fear self-nourishes, and the panic attack makes the individual feel he is plummeting towards the drama of his own death. Once the panic appears, it tends to repeat itself unrelentingly.

For those who experience a panic attack, instead of feeling reassured because they have survived and their terror is unfounded, they are increasingly inclined to let themselves be captured. In fact, it is often found that due to a hyperactivation of neurovegetative circuits, which send danger signals to consciousness, fear remains outside rational control. At a certain cognitive level, the patient 'knows' that he is not going to die, but at the same time he loses the ability to stem his fear and actually 'believes' he is going to die.

Although the panic attack is sudden, its preparation is long and it uses mental pathways and associations that tend to be employed repeatedly. The patient isolates some uncustomary signal (a palpitation, a muscular pain) and then, with a steady rise in anxiety, he constructs in his imagination the danger that triggers the terror. It is as if the catastrophic imagination were so powerful that it can capture the individual in a micro-delusion: the plane is going to crash, the lift is going to get stuck between two floors, and so on. Once the panic attack occurs, it constitutes a traumatic event, which is why it then continues to reoccur. When the mind is unable to contain the anxiety, this latter floods the body and becomes mortal panic. And so, the individual thinks: 'No, I am not anxious, I am really dying!'

As I mentioned earlier, Freud had already intuited back in 1894 that phobia and panic had a special status which placed them in the actual neuroses. We may say that here Freud had sensed the automatic and conditioned nature of panic anxiety that was caused by more primitive, automatic, and preverbal mechanisms and not by psychological factors. Freud's hypothesis of panic anxiety was set aside in subsequent psychoanalytic theories that sought to connect the panic attack to a specific conflictual pattern.

Many years later, another psychoanalytic paper that dealt in detail with phobia and panic attacks was that by Hanna Segal (1954), 'A note on schizoid mechanisms underlying phobia formation', in which she considered a patient with a severe phobic symptomatology and a probable borderline structure. Segal, who sought to place phobia within the concept of projective identification, began by assuming that the patient in question was fixed at the paranoid–schizoid position in which, as we know, projective and persecutory mechanisms are dominant.

A neuroscientific contribution

Neuroscientist Joseph LeDoux (1996) has identified two fear pathways: a simpler, faster, and less discriminating one, and another that is slower but more accurate.

The primitive circuit of fear, the simpler one, activates emergency signals that trigger immediate reactions such as fight or flight. This circuit belongs to the limbic system and is made up of the thalamus, the hypothalamus, the hippocampus, and the amygdala, this last being the most important control centre for danger signals. This system selects the coarser fear signals and incomplete stimuli associated to a danger and it then triggers hormonal and neurovegetative reactions connected to a fight or flight defence. What characterises this system is not so much its precision but its speedy and global action.

The second fear circuit runs from the prefrontal cortex to the limbic system. It is slower and more sophisticated, and, as such, enables a more attentive evaluation of the general situation before deciding on a response. Only at this point is there reflection, characterised by self-awareness, that is, consciously feeling fear and understanding why.

When we see a snake, the danger message goes to the visual cortex in the occipital lobe via the thalamus; then the prefrontal cortex is informed and it evaluates the level of danger posed by the stimulus by comparing it to learned or innate experiences; it then sends a signal to the amygdala, which in turn activates the automatic, neurovegetative, and biochemical innervations that produce fear reactions (increased heartbeat and breathing, vigilance, etc.).

The more discriminating and accurate thalamus–cortex–amygdala pathway is, however, too long to guarantee survival. So, the shorter pathway that goes directly to the amygdala in a few milliseconds triggers an immediate reaction to the danger. Let us consider a man who is walking in a wood at night, where any noise can set off an alarm reaction, triggering neurovegetative signals of fear. Only secondarily can it be understood whether the alarm was justified or not, as the alarm signal is activated along the shorter pathway, straight to the amygdala.

This faster pathway, which is not under the control of consciousness, has the drawback of possibly falsely recognising the danger; identifying the stimulus occurs afterwards, once the neurovegetative procession of fear has already been triggered.

Interesting is that the earliest alert to the object producing anxiety involves totally unconscious pathways that escape rational control; we may therefore assume that panic attack anxiety is trapped in the primitive fear (limbic–amygdala) circuit, which would explain its suddenness and non-discrimination between real and imagined danger.

For an individual who experiences a panic attack, *the imagined danger is equal to real danger*. That the panic reaction can be unbound from the real danger and be the effect of a construction by the imagination helps us understand the dissociation between real danger and imaginary danger, which is at the root of phobias and panic attacks. The amygdala can perceive imaginary constructions as danger signals.

A phobic individual creates a catastrophic scene in the mind that can become real; that scene is burnt into memory, becoming a traumatic nucleus that can produce terror. The panic attack, created by the imagination but felt concretely by the patient, is a real traumatic experience, and, as such, it is laid down as a traumatic memory.

The fear circuit can also be activated by perceptions of alarm coming from the body; for example, mild tachycardia can be registered as a sign of heart disease and turned into an actual heart attack. The body signal produces the panic attack, which continues to strike the body in an unbreakable vicious circle.

How can neuroscientific data and the psychoanalytic hypothesis of a panic attack as a symptom of a poorly structured self be brought together? How can it be explained that panic attacks disclose a deficit in areas of the personality and that they always accompany personal identity problems? Which defences collapse?

To address these questions, a few words are needed about defensive organisation in self-formation and its precariousness when identification with an idealised object in fantasy replaces self-awareness deriving from emotional experience. After presenting a case, this shall become clearer.

Panic and narcissistic defence

This twenty-five-year-old female patient began analysis at four sessions per week for repeated panic attacks and hypochondriacal episodes that constantly led her to doctors and the Accident and Emergency ward.

She was an intelligent and courageous child and teenager. During childhood, she never displayed yielding in situations where a child is normally in difficulty: she would go to the doctor without being afraid and tolerated physical pain well. On the threshold of early adulthood, this defensive cladding began to give: she was now afraid of everything and her imagination constantly constructed dangers and illnesses, including every kind of cancer.

In the first dream in analysis, the patient saw herself as a tourist guide while she was telling a group of people about sights in a city. She was aware in the dream of not knowing that city, nor anything about the sights she was showing. It is clear that she was showing the analyst how her falsified self had accompanied her when she was growing up, deluding herself and others into thinking she knew everything when she was perhaps totally ill-equipped to cope with life.

The patient's crisis, with the symptomatological procession that accompanies panic attacks, arose after her father's death and also after the break-up of a romantic relationship. This patient's alleged strength that had guided her in childhood and adolescence derived from an extremely idealised bond with her father, an important politician, who had made himself a role model to his daughter, who in turn was unable not to be strong and perfect.

One of this patient's characteristics, which is common to many individuals who suffer from panic attacks, is the need to live in the mind of the other and be seen ideally. She grew up as a 'courageous' girl because she had been dominated by a 'voice' that made her feel special when she coped well with danger and difficult situations. The courage that she was acknowledged to have had did not derive from real emotional competence, but from a need to hush that same 'voice' which was now accusing her of being a coward and a failure unless she faced risks. The more something was difficult and painful, the more she had to overcome fear in order to feel heroic. Important is that, in addition to the privileged relationship with her father, the maternal figure was absent, this little girl thus being left to face anxieties connected to the mysterious and disturbing functioning of the body and the external world all by herself.

Guided by her will to perform constantly, even in order to reassure her parents, the patient developed 'a second muscular skin' (Bick, 1968) in place of real abilities. She was a child expelled from both her parents' minds, thinking that she had to face everything alone.

Children like this feel evacuated by their mother and develop the thought of having to do everything by themselves, which naturally brings on anxiety at unbearable levels. In the case of this patient, her identity was closely connected to an illusory system that suddenly collapsed, leaving her in a state of terror.

This analysis ended well: the patient overcame her panic crisis after approximately one year of therapy when she became aware that she needed to acquire a true identity. Of extreme importance was going from an initial idealised transference, which referred to matters with her father, to a much more painful transference that was difficult to bear, in which affective dependence brought on a sense of desperate solitude. It was clear that the ideal bond the patient had constructed with her father had served to flee from the deficient relationship with her mother, which opened up again in full force in the transference during analytic separations. For a long time, there was continuous oscillation between an ideal relationship and a consequent collapse into solitude and desperation.

She overcame such oscillation by gradually understanding her past and by her introjection of a new object that could share emotions and support her. At this point, it was fundamental to analyse the illusory, seductive, and real elements in our relationship, and the consequent introjections of real experiences and bonds.

Therapy issues

Panic crisis therapy cannot be detached from pathological problems related to the sufferer's personality. There are more serious illnesses, borderline, for instance, which present with panic crises where the infantile-self disorder and the invasion of emotional space happened very early on and massively, at times as a consequence of violent projections from the parents. In these cases, trauma stunts psychological growth and severely distorts psychic development. Hidden self- or hetero-destructive elements determine a very shaky equilibrium and generate an emotional void and a lack of personal meaning that cannot easily be recovered. The panic symptom in these cases is prevalent and stubborn.

Analyses of this sort are the most complex and have the most uncertain outcome, where the inconsistency of positive life experiences cannot but repeatedly reproduce panic anxiety at length, while emotional growth proceeds with many oscillations and much difficulty.

In simpler cases, panic attacks signal the fall of narcissistic organisations, and for this reason they are particularly frequent in midlife crises (when the myth of one's efficiency, beauty, or success cannot sustain anxiety connected to the limit of one's existence), or in reactions to abandonment, when separating from one's partner is felt as a collapse of the self and one's self-confidence.

My viewpoint is that excitability and fantasy, which constitute a pleasant illusional world, are what create the catastrophic failure and plunge into nothingness. I am convinced that the imaginative structure which leads to traumatic terror after the fall of defences is an extension of the structure that erected the idealised self.

Panic attacks are also a tell-tale sign of a catastrophic crisis in one's inner world and one's defences, which, until a certain point, were able to prop it up. When panic is the effect of a narcissistic disorder, the situation is more favourable, as I have sought to illustrate in the case just described.

There are also some therapies in which the symptom weakens or vanishes in parallel to the treatment's positive development; it is as if the patient reaches a protected area, as a result of which the attacks end without the analyst or patient understanding why. This change usually derives from overcoming the constant state of emergency that prepares the panic attacks. It is likely that this change depends on a gradual transformational process that re-establishes a sufficient level of emotional vitality and allows the patient to leave the alarmed withdrawal in his body.

In cases, however, where the analysis is invaded by panic symptoms, two therapeutic needs must be met. The first is to help the patient control and understand his anxieties. Therapeutic work can help him bring to analysis experiences that precede the panic attack and it can describe how his imagination works. His fear is thus shared, and anxiety projection is facilitated, allowing the patient not to feel alone. This process helps contain and transform his anxiety.

The second need concerns the construction of a stable sense of self. Phobias and panic always reveal deficits in some important areas of the personality and go hand in hand with personal identity problems. This kind of patient does not know his emotions or how to deal with life's conflicts, and he is anxious and depressed. I think that his problems can be understood by taking into account how important his imagination has become (that is, broadly speaking, to include also daydreaming), as it has taken the place of consciousness for learning from experience.

Frequently, these patients are fragile, with a huge amount of imagination activity, including that which is narcissistic or dream-like, such as an ideal imagination of the self or promoting one's body. This means that the analysand must be helped to develop his own individuality and independently form opinions and thoughts, rendering his emotional experience free of inhibitions, self-praise, or unconditional agreement.

Conclusions

I have sought to consider ways in which a panic crisis develops based upon factors drawn from neuroscience and psychoanalytic clinical work.

My viewpoint is that somatic symptoms, whose origin is neurobiological, are not directly connected to conflict but rather to a basic psychological and emotional pattern marked by no anxiety containment. I believe, in fact, that the panic attack is an expression of the failure of those unconscious functions that modulate and monitor the emotional state.

The panic attack could also be hierarchically represented on three levels. The lowest, under the control of the amygdala, governs vegetative and somatic reactions. The intermediate level, that of traumatic memory, builds associations and visual and memory images that enter the catastrophic imagination. The uppermost level concerns personality structure, childhood experiences, and psychic defences, that is, a complex dynamic configuration that not only brings the symptom into being but also conditions the patient's whole inner and relational world.

The various therapies, each related to different aetiopathogenetic hypotheses, differ according to the level they act upon. At the lowest level, psychotropic medication is aimed at reducing the intensity of the neurovegetative reactions set off by the limbic system, as well as fighting the basic state of depression. Cognitive therapy, which addresses the intermediate level, seeks to correct perceptual distortions of fear via deconditioning strategies and gradual exposure to the stimulus that induces terror. Both approaches aim to rid the patient of the panic symptom.

Psychoanalytic therapy acts at a structural-dynamic level, not purely at a symptomatic level. As I mentioned a little earlier, at times, the panic symptom disappears spontaneously during the analytic process, whereas, at others, it persists and is destined to remain unchanged.

Clinical experience has convinced me that, in each case, it is essential to work on the panic attack *during the session*, examining it each time it manifests and inviting the patient to describe the feelings, perceptions, and thoughts that preceded and accompanied it. It is thus possible to recognise how the symptoms form, in which situations they are more likely to appear, and the role played by catastrophic imagination. This way, the patient has the chance to relive the traumatic event in the session; it can be shared with the analyst, analysed, and experienced in a potentially thinkable sequence.

This kind of analytic work enables the patient to take note of his own contribution to the construction of the attack. Consequently, new spaces and energy can be freed up for the development of the analytic process.

I would also like to underline that, the disappearance of symptoms aside, the path that leads to definitively overcoming the crisis can be fully achieved solely through the specific nature of the analytic process and the analysand's emotional growth.

CHAPTER 13

Trauma

The concept of trauma has been considered in a variety of ways by psychoanalytic thought, with its ebbs and flows affecting its definition and its prominence as a cause of illness.

Freud himself, who initially thought that sexual trauma was at the root of hysteria, subsequently retraced his steps and gave importance to psychic reality, that is, to the inner world built by the subject. The pathogenic effects of the 'real' external trauma thus moved into the background.

In one of his clinical cases (Freud, 1895d), he describes as follows his encounter with Katharina, an eighteen-year-old waitress who served him in a refuge hut while he was on an excursion in the mountains:

> 'Are you a doctor, sir? … I thought if you had a few moments to spare … The truth is, sir, my nerves are bad.' 'Well, what is it you suffer from?' 'I get so out of breath. But sometimes it catches me so that I think I shall suffocate.' 'Sit down here. What is it like when you get "out of breath"?' 'It comes over me all at once. First of all it's like something pressing on my eyes. My head gets so heavy, there's a dreadful buzzing, and I feel so giddy that I

almost fall over. Then there's something crushing my chest so that I can't get my breath.'

'And you don't notice anything in your throat?' 'My throat's squeezed together as though I were going to choke.' 'Does anything else happen in your head?' 'Yes, there's a hammering, enough to burst it.' 'And don't you feel at all frightened when this is going on?' 'I always think I'm going to die. I'm brave as a rule and go about everywhere by myself—into the cellar and all over the mountain. But on a day when that happens I don't dare to go anywhere; I think all the time someone's standing behind me and going to grab me all of a sudden.' (p. 281)

Freud commented: 'So it was in fact an anxiety attack, and introduced by the signs of a hysterical aura—or, more correctly, it was a hysterical attack the content of which was anxiety. Might there not probably be some other content as well?' (p. 281).

Continuing with the interview, Freud discovered that around the age of fourteen, this girl had been molested by her father, but that she had not experienced this parent's action as sexual aggression. Katharina added that she understood much later that it was something that was not quite right. She had also witnessed frequently the illicit sexual affair between her father and her female cousin. The anxiety that Katharina suffered during her attacks, Freud said, was hysteria resulting from sexual trauma. A distinctive feature of hysteria is that the symptoms do not manifest immediately after the trauma, but after a period of incubation. In this clinical account, Freud's initial conception of sexual trauma is clear, in that it is considered here in conventional terms, that is, in terms of sexual excitement, sexual impulse.

As just mentioned, the trauma does not produce immediate effects, since sexuality is dormant and repression in operation; subsequently, when sexuality is activated, sexual desire strengthened by the previous erotic experience that was endured emerges. The conflict between sexual desire and its denial provokes hysterical anxiety, which is no other than repressed sexual libido.

As can be seen, instead of taking into account the intrusiveness of adult sexuality in the childhood world, Freud concentrated on increased sexual excitation. This idea, in my opinion, explains some of

Freud's unsuccessful therapeutic outcomes. In the case of Dora (1905e), he tried to make the patient aware of her excitation in relation to Herr K.'s sexual advances, without considering this young adolescent's fear, and her refusal. Convinced by his sexual theory, Freud hoped that Dora would confirm it. Nausea, a symptom the patient complained of, corresponded to the displacement of sexual excitation from the genital organ to the mouth (aphonia, nausea) due to Dora's desire for oral intercourse. Freud considered it odd that a young fourteen-year-old girl would turn down a sexual advance by an adult, and he forwarded the hypothesis that Dora was unconsciously in love with Herr K. and had repressed this wish.

In *Studies on Hysteria* (1895d), there are two ways of understanding trauma: Freud's and Breuer's. Whereas Freud underlined the role of defence and repression (the affect is repressed and is therefore not conscious), Breuer emphasised the mechanism of vertical dissociation between conscious and unconscious states proposed by Janet (Craparo, Ortu, & Van der Hart, 2019).

Freud hypothesised a barrier between conscious and unconscious to safeguard consciousness from unconscious contents, defined as regressive in that they express primitive mental functioning. Breuer thought, however, that a traumatic experience did not get preserved in the unconscious, and instead it induced a state of autohypnosis (visible in Anna O.), which, befogging perceptions, prevented the individual from relating fully with reality.

Freud did not believe in autohypnotic hysteria, as he was convinced that childhood seduction in itself was not traumatic and was even possibly accompanied by pleasant feelings. The pathogenic power was connected to an overlap of pubertal sexual desires and memories of the childhood experience; guilt and shame, which trigger anxiety, then set repression in motion.

Breuer's point of view helps provide a better understanding of post-traumatic anxiety: the mental apparatus is unable to process the trauma and must therefore dissociate it, vertical *splitting* in consciousness consequently being needed. Befogged perception produced by autohypnosis causes a loss of contact with reality, ideas accountable for conversion waning on account of this. So, the trauma is 'remembered' in an altered state of consciousness and dissociated within the normal state of awareness.

The aetiological hypothesis linking neurosis to an excitatory sexual state was abandoned when Freud began to conceive psychic reality as separate from real experiences. The traumatic event occurred in fantasy due to sexual desires that originated in the Oedipus complex. Within this new perspective, the real external trauma was set aside, since what triggered anxiety was a fact imagined in fantasy.

The description of childhood neurosis in the clinical case of 'Little Hans' (1909b) marked the development of Freud's thought on trauma: trauma occurred in the inner world as a result of the impact of drives and a fear of punishment (the horse that frightened Little Hans tallied with the traumatising image of a castrating father).

The effect of real trauma on the psyche made a comeback during World War I, when Freud had to take into account the effects of war trauma.

In *Beyond the Pleasure Principle* (1920g), Freud used the term trauma descriptively, imagining a mind enclosed in a sort *of protective shield*, a barrier against excessive stimuli, which can be perforated by injury. In *Inhibitions, Symptoms and Anxiety* (1926d), he described some basic traumas, such as a loss of love from significant objects, maternal deprivation, and a loss of superego protection. For instance, in melancholy, the patient loses the love of the superego, which becomes a critical agency.

How can we define trauma?

Psychic trauma derives from a single or repeated event that proves detrimental, since the defences needed to understand and process it fall short. Some traumatic events will produce catastrophic effects at any age, but not all traumatic events will produce damage; in fact, the pathogenic effect of an event depends not only on its intensity, but on the individual's age and developmental stage, and what is damaging at one age may not be at a later age.

Environmental trauma

The concept of a protective shield, formulated by Freud within his economic model of the psychic apparatus, was then enriched by authors who stressed the importance of early childhood emotional experiences and environmental interference.

Among these authors, Ferenczi pointed out the ways in which a child's sensitivity and competence can be injured by adults when their own needs intrude upon a child's private area.

Balint (1968) spoke of a *basic fault*, something that happens in the first months of life, and which consists of traumatic breaches originating in a maternal inability to adapt to the child's basic needs. Effects of the emotional trauma manifest unpredictably some time afterwards.

One of the most important contributions to the conceptualisation of emotional trauma is certainly that provided by Winnicott (1965, 1971), who underlined the mother–child dual unit and the supportive environment. Winnicott hypothesised a potential developmental space since birth that can only be advanced within a sensitive encounter with a receptive mind. Continued trauma consists of no maternal containment, and, in extreme cases, of parents' projections of their own pathological psychic contents into the child's mind.

This type of trauma is clearly expressed in the concept of the *cumulative trauma* forwarded by Masud Khan (1963). The child's response to repeated maternal intrusions is psychological development distortions and inhibitions; moreover, if he perceives a parent's fragile areas, his vital aggressiveness is inhibited, or he develops a pseudo-mature false self.

Yet another author who has contributed enormously to our knowledge of the primitive mind and maternal containment is of course Bion, who spoke of a newborn, who needs to project his anxiety into his mother in order to survive.

What kind of mother is needed so that her child's emotional world can develop? A mother who is capable from the very beginning of accommodating fears, anxiety, and wishes that the child projects into her so that they are understood.

Bion (1992) called this operation projective identification for the purpose of communication. Personality development depends on the existence of an object with functions of the breast, into which the child can project his own projective identifications; if this object does not exist, there will be psychic disaster.

Both Winnicott and Bion thought that in order to live, every human being needed to use an object that could perceive and understand emotions, an object that was fit for his psychic development. If a mother (or an analyst) does not have receptive skills, the infant is destined to be unable to give meaning to his feelings and needs and will therefore not develop his world of emotions.

An object that can carry out 'dream work' for the child has been described by Bollas (1979) with the apt expression *transformational object*. The analytic process too depends on the analyst's ability to be a transformational object, and when this ability falls short, a psychoanalytic impasse can form, blocking the transformational process.

The contribution of neuroscience to memory systems

During the earliest stage of our life, traumatic experiences are not memorised, as this can be done only when we are able to represent and understand the meaning of an event.

Anne-Marie and Joseph Sandler (1987) theorised that we have a *past unconscious*, made up of a series of unconscious matters we cannot recall, and a *present unconscious*, which forms later and is based on representable emotional experiences. Only these representable experiences can be repressed and forgotten, that is, made unconscious and then go on to be recovered.

The Sandlers' intuitions have been confirmed by neuroscience, which distinguishes between *an explicit* and *an implicit memory*. Through the former, a forgotten event can be intentionally remembered, whereas implicit memory refers to that which has been learnt but cannot come into awareness since it concerns processes occurring very early on in life before our ability to represent has developed. It is hypothesised that the precursors to thought and affectivity, which are formed via processes outside awareness, can be disturbed in early infancy by traumatic events.

Following this line of thought, Fonagy (1999) maintains that borderline states derive from early traumas that were incorporated at a time before representation was possible. Borderline and psychotic patients are therefore unable to mentalize, that is, to represent emotions, psychic events, and mental states, the meaning of which they therefore ignore.

We can thus appreciate better Balint's intuition regarding early trauma, which is incorporated into the ego's structure, determining its malfunctioning.

Reassessing the concept of dissociation, some writings on the effects of sexual trauma (Davies, 1996) have shed new light on Breuer's contribution regarding the mechanism at work in his hysteria patients, which he had explained by vertical dissociation in consciousness.

From a certain viewpoint, we could say that Breuer more rightly suggested the concept of dissociation, proposed by Janet (Craparo, Ortu, & Van der Hart, 2019), in oneiroid states of hysteria patients (*la condition seconde*), whereas Freud had a general model of the unconscious in mind in which repression was the main defence. If, however, we look at the dynamics of severe psychopathologies and the condition of hysteria patients who were in therapy, we ought to recognise that Breuer's indication was more consistent with the psychopathological picture.

Dissociation, in fact, intervenes when repression cannot be used, or, rather, when anxiety levels are so high that they need to be dissociated. The part of the mind containing the traumatic memory is dissociated and thus the memory becomes inaccessible. Dissociation is considered a specific consequence of unbearable trauma, whereas repression is a process through which an experience that is relegated to the unconscious can be recovered once censorship has been lifted.

Helpful to understanding how traumatic memories become dissociated are neuroscientific studies on *explicit* or *declarative* memory and *implicit* or *procedural* memory.

These two types of memory are situated in two different brain systems, and they differ from a developmental as well as an anatomical viewpoint. Explicit memory depends on the hippocampus, whose bilateral destruction results in an inability to memorise an event. The emotional component, fear and anxiety in particular, is registered in the amygdala. Implicit memory depends on the basal ganglia and the cerebellum (Levin, 2009). This neurophysiological memory structure enables us to understand what happens in a traumatic event.

Traumatic memories are encoded by the brain differently from other memories. LeDoux (1996) maintains that due to amygdala excitation, fear memories are burnt into memory. The amygdala, which is part of the primitive circuit of fear and poorly connected to cortical circuits, registers a trauma and keeps it within the primitive circuit, without affording it any chance of transformation. By so doing, the conscious memory of the traumatic event is weak if not altogether absent, whereas the emotional memory reactivates when there is a stimulus connected to the trauma.

The effects of a traumatic event in current psychiatric nosography come under post-traumatic stress disorder (PTSD). One feature of this disorder is a constant repetition of the traumatic event: as opposed to being forgotten, the unpleasant event is continuously repeated. To cancel the threatening anxiety, the mental apparatus creates a dissociation in consciousness, and the traumatic feelings are relived not as an ordinary memory but as affective states, somatic feelings, and visual images that experience cannot change.

Psychoanalytic thought took up theorising trauma and dissociation again after a lull. Dissociation re-emerged when several severe psychopathological patterns (Vietnam War veterans with PTSD, and sexual abuse victims) were taken into consideration.

According to modern psychoanalytic perspectives, from Bion onwards, repression is not solely a defence but also a mechanism that allows lived experience to become unconscious. Were there not repression, emotional content would linger in consciousness without ever being dreamt or transformed into thought. Only what has been *digested* can be forgotten, such as dreams, which serve to integrate thoughts, permitting them to be forgotten.

In dissociation, what is dissociated is a part of the mind, the traumatic memory that can no longer be accessed. Traumatic anxiety, which connects back to impotence and terror experienced in solitude, is not *thinkable* and must be denied; it does continue to live on in dissociated memory, though.

Sexual abuse and sexualisation

In writings on sexual abuse, defensive aspects that lead to dissociating the trauma from consciousness are usually what is focused on. Less frequently do we find a description of psychopathological structures that can develop following sexual abuse. When children abused by psychotic mothers are in therapy, they tend to sexually seduce the therapist openly. This behaviour confirms Freud's primitive hypothesis that sexual abuse can set in motion unconscious sexual excitation in a child.

Karl Abraham (1907) put forward a description of the process of sexualisation that can occur following sexual trauma. By observing that sexual abuse was found more frequently in ill individuals, with neurosis or psychosis, Abraham hypothesised that some children prematurely reach sexual pleasure and for this reason they are able to frequent abusing adults without having excessive defences. Prematurely encountering sexuality indicates that disruptive developmental elements are already active. Abraham therefore envisioned a reverse sequence in which sexualised withdrawal preceded and facilitated trauma. Trauma would therefore not be the *primum movens* of psychopathological development, but a symptom of a situation that was already abnormal. For Abraham, infantile sexual trauma played no aetiological role in hysteria or psychosis; rather, it expressed a predisposition in infancy to subsequent neurosis or psychosis.

Early relational trauma

If a patient's history is woven with childhood traumatic experiences, these will continually re-emerge in analytic work, through anxiety and the transference, but also dreams. For this reason, the analyst must keep the patient's disturbing emotional environment in mind, so that a good enough emotional setting for that patient's specific story can be provided.

The clinical issue does not solely depend on the direct effects of the trauma, but also, and above all, on the indirect effects, that is, on the cluster of individual responses in the form of psychopathological structures that the trauma set in motion.

It is important to remember that variables which interfere with development do not solely depend on possible inadequate or distorted responses from primary objects, but also on the child's subjective readiness to create defences or psychopathological structures that go on to acquire major significance over time.

A very effective illustration of early emotional trauma was given by Green (1980) in his paper *The Dead Mother*, in which he analysed the effect of maternal depression on a child. A maternal figure that is physically present but mentally absent is a psychic catastrophe for her child. One of the most frequent outcomes is that the child will identify with his mother and that, following massive radical disinvestment, a psychic hole will form in place of the absent object. Loss of meaning then follows on from loss of love, and a sense of self, unsupported by maternal empathy, will not develop. Following this line of thought, Green closely connected the infantile traumatic experience and psychopathology development in adulthood.

Trauma in the primary relationship

By *emotional trauma*, or *trauma in the primary relationship*, I am referring to the set of distorted responses that can psychopathologically condition a child's development.

In severely disturbed patients, it is not so much a case of emotional absence as it is the intrusion of the primary object's ill, superegoic, or confused parts. Taken into the self are parts of the object, thus creating a pathological identification with an invasive object that goes on to form part of the child's self (Williams, 2004). In this case, we therefore find ourselves dealing with an internalised object that has become part of the patient; in the more complex pathologies, these introjected objects work against the patient, at times seducing him, at times intimidating him, but above all, confusing him.

Williams thinks that a pathological parent can intrude into the child's mind to rid himself of excited or plainly ill parts he is unable to keep inside. The child thus becomes a container of his parent's ill parts and loses the perception of being a separate person. Once identification with the ill parent has occurred, the child feels as if he has an intrusive object inside and, at the same time, that he is invaded by alien and incomprehensible external objects.

In disorganised attachment behaviour during early childhood, attachment theory has identified the precursor to psychopathological structures and *dissociation* in adulthood.

A serious lack of physical or emotional protection by parents, or ill-treatment and abuse during childhood, especially when carried out by caregiving figures, or dysfunctional styles in the relationship with the mother, are traumatic and determine recurrent experiences of overwhelming threat from which there is no escape. When a child is deprived of his parents' indispensable protection or that of other adults, or when their presence turns into a source of alarm or danger, fear with no way out is produced, preventing the child from coherently organising normal attachment behaviour.

Reconstructing trauma

The importance we give to emotional trauma in the primary relationship impacts directly on our way of listening to patients; one function of analytic listening is to distinguish between what was created by the infantile trauma and what depends on psychopathological structures. The manner in which emotional trauma/psychopathological development interweave will enable the analyst to intuit how complex the therapeutic course of each single case will be.

Although the emotional trauma will have affected personality structure, causing anxiety and developmental arrests and creating psychopathological structures, a part of unconscious perceptive functions will still be there and in operation: the analyst must address these.

As I have mentioned, in more developed (neurotic) patients who can represent, trauma in the primary relationship is expressed in some dreams where the analyst can appear in place of the past traumatic object. These dreams, with an apparent transference meaning, describe very well the nature of the traumatic relationship with the past object.

In the more complex mental disorders, it is important to distinguish between pathological structures that originated in early intrusion by the primary objects and those that involve the patient's active construction.

What jumps out at us in some cases is not traumatic suffering proper, but a complete lack of the mind getting structured throughout childhood.

If a child lives in a world without emotional responses from his parents, he will be unable to develop representations that are fundamental to establishing his sense of reality. At times, a parent's psychic absence can favour pleasant flight into the world of imagination to the detriment of contact with psychic reality; this is one of the reasons why a number of patients, despite having had a traumatic childhood, are totally unaware of it.

I believe that two equally important factors, which are destined to reinforce one another, contribute to fostering psychopathology in more complex patients: a lack of environmental empathy, and psychopathological structure construction by the child himself, leading to deviation from normal development.

Trauma and victimistic withdrawal

Whereas some patients have no awareness of having suffered emotional childhood traumas, which usually only emerge at an advanced stage of analysis, other patients speak of their traumas from the very beginning of therapy. A thorough description is given of their parents' character, including their failings, and any injustices the patient has suffered. It is as if these patients have taken note of all the wrongs, both inevitable and sporadic, for the excitement of a mental refuge that is laden with resentment and violence. The analyst's emotional participation fails to comfort them and may even add fuel to their string of complaints; amidst their reports of past suffering, the figure of the victim gets nourished and mounting aggressiveness develops.

John Steiner (1993) maintains that specific pathological organisations are at the root of this *resentment* and *rancour*, which can be seen as passive, masochistic, or maniacal defences, deriving from intolerable guilt. Chronically feeling a victim of injustice serves the purpose of not calling into question one's own responsibility and not working through the mourning of the trauma or of what was lost in the past and can no longer be retrieved. Traumatic suffering is transformed into chronic warfare in which the object is attacked and real separateness is never reached; perverse satisfaction that is gained via excitement in a counter-aggressive loop makes change increasingly difficult.

I have sought to describe a series of concatenations between the traumatic experience (especially when early), memory, and effects on the growing individual. As can be seen, it is a very complex interweave.

A frequent viewpoint in contemporary literature tends to consider all experiences that disturb affective infantile development as traumatic, especially those relationships in which the mother does not respond empathically to the child's requests for emotional contact or to his need for containment and the structuring of his mind.

Among empathic responses are the right frustrations, not to be considered as traumatic, since they serve to structure the mind. A mother must know how to distinguish between her child's needs and his claims for control. Frustrations in this case serve to contain omnipotence and lend substance and structure to the child's personality. Often noted in psychopathology is a mix of deficiencies and privileges that accompanied growth: the sum of these often produces disastrous results.

CHAPTER 14

Identity and psychopathology

In this chapter, I shall try to cast light on similarities and differences in identity disorders and depersonalisation in various clinical syndromes as well as describe the main psychopathological mechanisms in neurotic and borderline conditions; lastly, I shall formulate some hypotheses on depersonalisation in the psychotic process.

Identity is what makes us unique, with a name, an appearance, and a mindset that is ours. We preserve the illusion of staying the same in a continuous transformation that shapes us over the years, from childhood to adolescence, and from adulthood to old age.

Our uniqueness is also linked to the group we belong to. We recognise ourselves in others we feel are similar to us, but are aware of our differences, too.

Experiencing the self, which we do from birth, enables us to live our body distinctly from that of others; this experience can be considered as the first and most basic manifestation of identity. Our ego, as Freud had anticipated, is therefore first and foremost a bodily ego.

Winnicott (1965) was the first psychoanalyst to formulate a genetic hypothesis of the self, a subjective experience of being in the world that develops in parallel to mental functions.

The starting point for the emotional development of subjectivity is the early period in which the mother mirrors the child and can identify with him and his wishes and needs. A consistent sense of reality, which our security and our mental wellbeing are founded upon, is based on our earliest relations with an adult who can acknowledge us and return to us the significance of our personal uniqueness.

Recent studies, especially in infant research, have confirmed Winnicott's intuitions: the foundations of individual consciousness are structured during our preverbal period before we are able to represent.

Among the many contemporary contributions on preverbal processes that structure the early nucleus of the self, I shall cite that of Beebe, Lachmann, and Jaffe (1997). Reciprocal interactions between mother and child during the first year of his life organise subjectivity and create patterns that will go on to make up unconscious organising structures on which personality and identity are based. These authors believe that the newborn's representations are symbolised above all in the nonverbal representation system and that they belong to memory which cannot access awareness.

In other words, emotional functions implied in identity formation develop at the beginning of life when the infant's nonverbal emotional communication is adequately understood and returned by the mother. A parent's ability to attribute to the child intentionality, and to consider him endowed with thoughts and wishes, is therefore central to establishing his sense of identity.

Fonagy et al. (2003) too sustain that interiorising a parent's affective response enables the infant to develop representations of his own mental state, and, consequently, to structure the nucleus of his self as an intentional agent. To develop a sense of identity, the child needs another mind that registers his feelings and intentions, but which does not invade him (above all with negative affects). A mother must understand the infant's emotion and return it so that he can interiorise his emotional state that has been enriched with meaning. It is important that communication indicates to the child that what he sees is a reflection of his own feelings and not his mother's.

Some neuroscientific data

The above observations can be integrated with those of neuroscientists, who tell us that self-awareness depends on unconscious cognitive processes. In this regard, neuroscience speaks of *implicit aspects of the self*, that is, aspects of what we are that are not available to consciousness and because of their nature are inaccessible. Both implicit and explicit knowledge contribute to forming the perception of self-unity, which is never in a stable form.

Over recent years, attention, memory, and consciousness have become areas of investigation for neuroscience. As for identity, neuroscientists think that self-perception is the result of an integration of many independent functional structures. The most important of these are: an awareness of one's own body, expressed through our certainty that it has always belonged to us; self-memories (autobiographical memory); and the perception of one's own space, which is organised around a personal core, enabling us to perceive ourselves as separate from others.

Studies using neuroimaging techniques which investigate self-recognition (our awareness of being within a body in a particular space) and self-reflection (the ability to consider one's being as an object of investigation and to direct attention towards inner thoughts, memories, emotions, and visceral feelings) has highlighted the crucial role of several brain structures.

One brain region involved in these tasks is the *medial prefrontal cortex*, situated in the fissure between both hemispheres; it coordinates and integrates all perceptions and memories that contribute to creating the unitary perception of who we are (Gusnard et al., 2001).

A second strategic area is the *precuneus*, part of the parietal lobe that connects to the right posterior parietal cortex, the hippocampus, and medial prefrontal areas; it is involved in self-awareness via the recall of autobiographical memories (Lou et al., 2004; Johnson et al., 2006).

A third structure is the *anterior insula*, a cortical area situated below the temporal lobes, which enables information about an individual's characteristics to be differentiated from such information about others (Zimmer, 2005).

The brain areas described here (the medial prefrontal cortex, the precuneus, and the anterior insula) connect up to the hippocampus and other older structures (Damasio, 2010) to form the neuronal structure that supports personal identity perception.

It is highly likely that these structures operate constantly with those involved in organising a theory of mind (Baron-Cohen, 1987), that is, an ability to infer the functioning of others' and one's own mind.

In other words, only when we come to understand that others have their own intentions and thoughts can we obtain a separate sense of identity.

Using functional magnetic resonance imaging (fMRI), Northoff et al. (2006) studied the 'self-reference effect', that is, the relationship between memories and emotions that the subject has personally experienced and which have left a specific trace, and other events that are not characterised so. Brain regions specifically involved in processing emotions and faces were highlighted in this study. These regions do not show a difference between specific and non-specific stimuli for the self; only in other brain areas (the anterior cingulate cortex, the prefrontal cortex, and the precuneus, for instance) is a difference noted for stimuli related to the self and those not specific to the self. In general, the cortical midline structures seem to have special significance for the self and self-reference.

Another contribution that helps us to understand identity is that by Edelman (1992), who put forward a distinction between *primary consciousness* and *higher-order consciousness*.

Primary consciousness enables us to have partial awareness of things in our world, such as mental images of the present, but no feeling of being a person with a past or a future. Made up of phenomenal experiences and bound to time in the measurable present, primary consciousness does not include past or future, but has only a small memory interval which Edelman called the *remembered present*. This does not mean that an animal with primary consciousness only cannot have a long-term memory or act on the basis of this; clearly, it can, but in general it is unaware of that memory, and it does not represent its future.

Higher-order consciousness, instead, enables us to recognise our actions and feelings; it includes a model of personal identity, a present, a past and a future, and it indicates direct and reflective awareness of mental episodes that happen without the involvement of sense organs or receptors. To perceive a sense of personal identity, we need language and a use of symbols, which belong to higher-order consciousness.

For Edelman, involved in self-awareness is the subjective perception of emotions.[3]

---

[3] 'Higher-order consciousness depends on building a Self through affective intersubjective exchanges ... Tragedy becomes possible—the loss of the Self by death or mental disorder, the remembrance of unassuageable pain' (Edelman, 1992).

Higher-order consciousness (the self in psychoanalysis) frees up thought from constraints in the immediate present and permits reflective perception of our existence and emotional continuity.

Animals endowed with primary consciousness are unable to interiorise time through affective cognition; their experience therefore remains connected to a concrete succession of events that are not experienced in emotional time.

Physiological identity crises

If our sense of identity has extremely early origins in the close relationship with the maternal figure, then the emotional and cognitive experiences that can be added to and integrated into this primitive nucleus are many.

As we know, our sense of identity, which changes and consolidates over our lifetime, can go through moments of change that often present themselves as existential crises.

An important moment of transformation is without a doubt the adolescent crisis. This is a time in life when old affective objects and our bonds with them go through crisis. An adolescent needs to look for a new identity that is different from his childhood one, which was built within the dependence relationship with his parents, and in order to do so, he takes up a rebellious position. Passing from familiar childhood love objects to adult objects outside the family is closely connected to an *exogamus need*, which is the most extreme request to break our bonds with primary objects (Fornari, 1966). This change of direction is bound to provoke a sort of *abrupt and ambiguous reorganisation* of identity, with fast and complex attitude changes. A relational tempest occurs with great force and determination in the more vital adolescents, who feel they can throw previous relationships into crisis without incurring a loss of the self. Others, who instead feel their self is threatened, risk staying in a relationship where they submit to the old objects without facing up to the necessary transformational crisis because of their fragile and vulnerable self.

Another significant identity crisis occurs in middle age, the famous *midlife crisis* (Jaques, 1965), which takes place between the ages of forty and fifty and brings with it instability that varies from one individual to the next. This is the age at which a person stops growing and starts to become old, and defences, which until then had been helpful, turn out to be unsuitable for dealing with the last part of one's life.

The perception of one's life's limits is no longer a general concept or an experience that belongs to someone else: it becomes a personal matter, as it concerns one's own mortality. A midlife crisis can be overcome if the limit of existence and the traumatic impact of the thought of one's death can be dealt with constructively.

Pathological disorders of personal identity are marked by their phenomenology, but also their consequences. Generally speaking, it is important to differentiate between a temporary failing of self-cohesion, following trauma or transient depersonalisation, as occurs in neurotic conditions (panic attacks, for instance), and *structured identity disorders* in severe pathologies, in which a sense of personal identity presents with discontinuity and fractures that cannot be easily reversed.

Neurotic depersonalisation

Individuals who suffer from depersonalisation experience an alteration to the perception of the body and the psychic self in that they no longer feel their body or parts of it as their own, and they experience a sense of unreality. This last-mentioned perception is quite frequent in hysterical and depressive disorders, and although distressing, it is not long-lived. At times, depersonalisation has the same characteristics as panic attacks, which, as I mentioned in Chapter 12, are accompanied by considerable neurovegetative manifestations.

In particular, the feeling of being contained in the safe marked-out space of one's body disappears. In panic attacks, psychological and biological mechanisms intersect and reciprocally strengthen one another.

The crisis, whose preparation is rather long, is characterised by depression that goes unnoticed by the patient himself, who feels in a constant state of alarm with no defences. Somatic symptoms are connected to a basic psychological and emotional constellation in which anxiety containment breaks down.

A fragile self's lack of defences opens the gates to an anxiety surge. But it is the identity defect that causes the collapse of the 'self'.

Depersonalisation in the borderline state

A frequent and dramatic characteristic of therapy with borderline patients is the sudden violence directed against others, and, more often, against themselves. Self-harming, which is carried out with incredible determination, often follows episodes of emotional frustration. During therapy, it is difficult to reconstruct with these patients the act of self-harm, which is triggered by unbearable tension. Borderline patients, as they fall into a state of non-existence, must exit from it at all costs: 'like I'm not there, like I'm not real. When I start to cut-up and see the blood … it ends. I'm back inside myself' (Miller & Bashkin, 1974, pp. 640–641).

In this article by Miller and Bashkin (1974), published in *The Psychoanalytic Quarterly*, I found a vivid description of these dynamics. They wrote of a young, severely traumatised male patient who, during therapy, had three episodes of self-mutilation, all connected to emotional traumas, such as changing his therapist or his residential home, or abandonment by a girl. When describing his episodes of self-violence, the sequence was always the same: not feeling real and cutting himself to feel real again. At the start of the episode, he would feel depressed, and seemed to get swallowed up by a dark cloud that made him feel unreal. Then, he would begin to cut himself to come out of this state of depersonalisation.

This situation, which is not infrequent during therapy with borderline patients, is something that every therapist fears: after feeling frustration, the patient unleashes violence on emotional aspects of his self, which are punished for having exposed him to suffering.

In this regard, Rosenfeld (1978) hypothesised that early childhood trauma, including physical trauma, together with a lack of maternal empathy, can create a concentration of anger and desperation. In these situations, aggressiveness is directed at the libidinal self, which is attacked because the patient feels that this alive part of the self is responsible for his suffering. Confusion between the libidinal and destructive parts is responsible for states of emptiness and passivity, which lead to a death wish, disappearing into nothingness, a condition that is frequently found in borderline patients.

This effect is catastrophic because violence against the emotional apparatus also brings about a disappearance of the self, which is dragged into the agony of non-existence. At this point, only the sight of blood and pain are proof that the patient is not dead, a feeling that comes about due to a total absence of self-vitality.

Agnese is a fifteen-year-old girl who began therapy two years earlier because of considerable difficulties: her performance at school came to a halt, she tended to isolate and have sudden fits of psycho-motor agitation similar to panic attacks, but which turned out to be hysterical. During her therapy, Agnese's behaviour improved, as did her studies and human relationships. Starting from this newfound wellbeing, Agnese took a leap forward when she fell in love with a girl in her class, with whom she formed an exclusive relationship. She then broke it off and began another, which turned out to be stormy. This second partner then left her to begin a heterosexual relationship with a boy their age. Agnese then began to cut her tummy (there had been similar episodes previously). During this period, she brought a dream that clarified the dynamics of these acts of cruelty. In the dream, she is with a man armed with a knife, who is going to attack the two girls she was attached to. When the man raises his arm to strike them, Agnese steps between them to protect the girls and is injured on her tummy.

The sadomasochistic bond Agnese has with her traumatic objects is evident, as is her desire for revenge and her yielding to a masculine narcissistic organisation which dominates her; in the end, she carries out violence against the tender, helpless part of her body and self.

Depersonalisation in the psychotic state

Anna, one of my first psychotic patients, began psychoanalytic therapy as soon as she was discharged from hospital; she had been admitted due to a delusional episode, initially erotic in nature and then persecutory.

After the initial interviews, it was not difficult to agree a traditional analytic setting with her at four weekly sessions. Unlike the period of time she had spent in hospital, where worry had not come into the picture, once at home again she became very pained. Her sessions were a scarce resource for the intensity of her anxiety. Having returned to the real world and having had to be back in touch with life made her totally lose her bearings. Her greatest difficulties were when she woke up and would find it extremely hard to get out of bed. She told me that she would light a cigarette and while smoking it would dream of being a sheikh surrounded by a troupe of Indian dancing-girls. She thus reached ecstatic pleasure, which collapsed, however, when she left this mental state; she felt depersonalised and prey to panic, remembering nothing about herself or the world. The patient spoke of these mental states as 'psychic infarctions'.

I have mentioned this clinical fragment as it seems suited to introducing the topic of losing the self in psychosis.

This patient's depersonalisation, 'psychic infarction', was preceded by her carrying out a mental operation that, despite originating as a defence against anxiety, submerged her in a pleasant sensorial withdrawal that meant her losing her personal identity. Once outside the withdrawal, she was left with no connection at all between her self and psychic reality.

Psychotic functioning alters a patient's sense of reality, projecting him into an omnipotent or persecutory world and distorting his original identity. From this radical upheaval of psychic reality derives the loss of the self that is typically found in this illness.

Psychotic development

A particularly dramatic phenomenon during psychotic depersonalisation is the loss of psychic skin. One of my patients would say that he 'had lost his armour' in order to explain that he could not catch a train because he felt penetrated by the looks and bodies of passengers in his compartment.

Losing one's psychic skin follows a state of grandiosity, which brings with it the danger of disintegration and the loss of one's real identity. Overcome by the flow of all possible sensory feelings that invade him, the patient feels like a log, a raft transported by a swift, swollen river, at the mercy of the current and the power of others. When taking on the identity of another, creating excitement inside him, he does not realise that the delusion is an attack on his own identity. He is unaware that this operation wipes out his own identity, the only identity that would allow him to be in his own skin and maintain a reassuring distance from the world that surrounds him.

In a withdrawal, mechanisms are created that alter psychic reality and personal identity via a pathological identification with grandiose and omnipotent characters created in fantasy. At work is the mechanism of projective identification described by Klein (1946). The characters, having become concrete and real, are what mix with residual fragments of the patient's *real identity*, producing confusion and depersonalisation.

My hypothesis is that depersonalisation phenomena are the outcome of a prolonged distortion that the psychotic individual creates in his own mind. Instead of using his mind as an organ of consciousness to communicate with people, the psychotic patient uses it as an instrument with which to create feelings that take him to a type of special but regressive pleasure. Depersonalisation occurs when realities that are built in the dissociated world begin to invade the perception of emotional and psychic reality. Areas marked by confusion between what is real and what has been falsified in the psychic withdrawal are thus created. This confusion does not only affect the perception of external reality (*derealisation*) but also, and above all, the individual's identity, to the extent that the patient's biographical history is altered (*depersonalisation*).

In the psychotic process, anxiety linked to a loss of self is also unleashed when the capture of the healthy part by the psychotic part reaches its peak. At this point, the perception of irreversible psychic catastrophe emerges. This is the anxiety that characterises the phenomenology of *Wahnstimmung*, which for last century's psychiatry constituted the dramatic beginning of the psychotic process. This is the moment when depersonalisation reaches its highest level.

In this regard, Bion (1967) stated the following:

> The patient feels imprisoned in the state of mind he has achieved, and unable to escape from it because he feels *he lacks the apparatus of awareness of reality* [my italics] which is both the key to escape and the freedom itself to which he would escape. (p. 39)

In other words, when the psychotic patient becomes imprisoned in his delusional false identity, he is no longer equipped with the apparatus of awareness of reality, the only means that could help him rebuild his real identity. Leaving the psychotic withdrawal to face psychic reality therefore becomes a catastrophic depersonalising experience.

Differentiating neurotic and psychotic depersonalisation

One difference between neurotic and psychotic depersonalisation concerns the degree of reversibility. Although felt particularly dramatically, depersonalisation phenomena in neurosis are always limited in time. They occur following a break in the emotions' container due to the fragility of the apparatus sustaining identity. Indeed, these patients often live in a fantasy world that weakens real identity. They are impressionable, wary, and unable to be confidently in contact with psychic reality, seemingly having developed what in psychoanalytic literature is referred to as a false self (Deutsch, 1955; Winnicott, 1965).

Depersonalisation in borderline patients is the result of the personality's alive parts being suppressed, the individual experiencing this as an anxious feeling of non-existence. The patient must rid himself of psychic death but needs to do so employing violent methods. No thoughts are there to deal with the paralysis, so the skin, the sheath containing the self, needs to be cut, allowing the patient at that point to come out of his deadly prison.

Depersonalising anxiety in psychosis is instead the consequence of a psychic withdrawal the patient has found refuge in (as in Anna's case). As long as the patient stays in his sensory refuge, the pleasantness of this condition will keep all anxiety at bay, but once the protection of this created fantasy world fails, anxiety is unleashed.

CHAPTER 15

Melancholic depression

Depressive disorders, which we see so frequently, present with a wide variety of clinical pictures.
In this chapter, I shall try to summarise Freud's and Abraham's theories on depression, looking specifically at the dynamics of the melancholic depressive state. I shall then look at emptiness, suffering, a loss of meaning and a lack of a life project in the following chapter. These are found in non-melancholic depression and are frequently associated with other symptoms such as panic attacks and phobias.

A patient

This is the case of a female patient with melancholic depression.

This lady is forty-nine years old, married with a son, has been hospitalised several times for depression and has undergone electroconvulsive therapy. She only spoke to me about this, though, after several months of analysis, for fear she would be considered too severe a case and therefore refused therapy.

Relations with her husband are not good: despite continuing to live together, there has been no affective relationship for quite some time, and sexual relations stopped many years ago.

It seems that the patient married for social convenience. Her husband is very wealthy and matches the expectations of the patient's mother, who insisted upon her daughters marrying wealthy men to raise their social level from the petty bourgeoisie they were born into.

The patient began analysis, as she was later to understand, because she was distressed about the likelihood of an extramarital romantic bond coming to an end, and she feared facing the second part of her life bearing a profound sense of guilt and destruction. With her fiftieth birthday approaching, her son, whom she is totally devoted to, decided to leave home.

A dream after the first sessions provides a very clear picture of this patient's existential crisis and lack of meaning in her life. She dreams of being in a Mediterranean city and getting arrested for being too elegant. She finds herself in a street that leads who knows where; she sees the last building, a church, which is just a façade, like a theatre prop. The patient associates the church with her marriage and the town with the one she went to on honeymoon.

In the dream, the patient provides a picture of herself and the conflict she finds herself in: she acknowledges that her marriage is only a façade, while her superego condemns her for wanting to be too elegant. The patient is very beautiful, rich, and elegant, and the accusation in the dream points to her narcissism.

Several months into her analysis, the patient learns that her husband is having an affair with another woman. This fills her with anger and makes her attempt suicide. It then forces her to separate from her husband, despite this not being what she wants. She does not want to make up with a man she does not love, towards whom she only feels vengeful anger. Ultimately, the patient feels she is a victim of her husband and bears no responsibility for her failed marriage: her infidelities do not count.

A sadomasochistic relation soon takes shape within the analytic relationship: the patient accuses me of countless shortcomings, cruelty, and failings, and often sternly lectures me. I am constantly challenged about times, holidays, and payment for sessions. The analytic setting is a system imposed upon her by a domineering analyst who behaves cruelly towards her. If I interpret, I do so to make her feel horrible, and if I am silent, it is because I want to humiliate her. She experiences me as someone who wishes to deprive her of her pleasures and make her adopt a monastic lifestyle. It is clear that the patient ascribes to me an ascetic ideal that I want to impose upon her against her will.

Clearly, the patient is engaging in an extremely cruel relationship with me, attributing sadistic blame to the object.

In the countertransference, I can feel unwonted difficulty experiencing warm and friendly feelings; I realise that the patient is unable to tolerate guilt and needs to project it into me. My position is difficult. Invested by all negative qualities, in turn I also have to deal with feelings of rejection. The risk is that of re-projecting cruelty into the patient by making interpretations on her destructiveness, which would be disastrous. In fact, were I to do it, I would become incorporated into the patient's sadistic superego, and risk repeating (in the transference and the countertransference) relational patterns of her previous years; a sort of relationship similar to that between two people who constantly row and level accusations at each other would form, just as it had with her parents and then her husband.

In our analytic work, a sort of inner accusing voice comes through. Internally, the patient is made to feel guilty by a parent reprimanding her for being devoid of love and unable to be constructive, as is clear in her first dream where she is arrested and charged with being too elegant.

This inner experience originated in the patient's relationship with her father, whom she experienced as her only parent of worth. Her mother was hysterical and primitive, and despite being affectionate at times, she was insensitive; she would frequently throw sudden and unpredictable fits of rage, was hysterically depressed, and dependent on her husband. The patient's father had pushed his daughter to proceed with her studies, bringing positive and constructive input to her life, but their relationship was a very complex one.

Towards the third year of analysis, the patient remembers an erotic episode with him. She is convinced that she seduced her father, even though she remembers that he really admired her youthful beauty. Frequently, she heard her father praising her beauty when speaking to his wife, the patient's mother.

Even when I try to convey the idea that perhaps it was her father who took the initiative, the patient's superego convinces her it was the other way round. Only later, when she learns that her sister too suffered the same treatment by their father, does she accept my assumption.

The patient distanced herself from her mother and during her adolescence began to idealise her father. Not having been attributed any real significance by her mother, her father had, by idealising her back, helped construct her narcissism: self-praise derived from this, followed by denigration.

Frequently during this period, a contradictory and befuddling superegoic object appears in the patient's dreams, exalting her by making her feel special to then attack and denigrate her. This object generates uncertainty and confusion: on the one hand, the superego attacks and denigrates her (the melancholic pole), and on the other, it exalts her (the maniacal pole). For example, during her separation from her husband, in the patient's mind there is a constant toing and froing between a vision of herself as a woman who is being humiliated by her spouse, and an egotistical woman who is abandoning her son and husband.

In the transference, the ascetic and spiritual analyst is set against an image of a seducer who exalts her. And in a dream in which I appear with a sort of Bohemian hat, I represent an uncle who used to take her to the cinema and the theatre, treating her like a princess.

Slowly, the atmosphere, charged with excitement and persecution, begins to tone down, and the patient is able to experience a better relationship with the world; not feeling solely full of envy and vindictive desires, she brings a reparative-type dream.

In the dream, she is looking at her hands and realises that her hand is better, even though a finger is missing, her ring finger, which had been seriously injured. The patient associates it with her brother, who, after the end of the war, found an explosive device in their garden and had to have a finger amputated.

In the dream, the patient identifies with her brother, says that 'something has remained', and that she can use the other fingers on her hand. Associations lead her to her failed marriage and to her feelings towards her husband that are no longer aggressive. Light is also cast on her regret for what she feels she lost in her past because her fickle and false part had dominated. It comes through that this part colonised her personality and her self-constructive part. This perception makes a more balanced assessment possible as well as greater appreciation of her more authentic parts.

Abraham's conceptualisation

For Abraham, important to the origin of the melancholic structure is infantile trauma. He wrote about this in his essay on Segantini (1911), when he stated that this artist harboured a fascination for death because of early maternal abandonment.

In the case of my patient, the trauma was her difficult relationship with her mother, who had not helped her grow up, and the patient then turned to her father, idealising him.

Another significant factor causing this illness, according to Abraham, was the melancholic's narcissistic structure. Abraham placed melancholy at an oral-sadistic level, that is, at a primitive stage of psychosexual development. Yet another important point concerned the action of the superego, our moral conscience, which accuses the patient of being bad or a failure, as well as the sadistic-aggressive aspect of the object relation. In all his writings on melancholy, Abraham stressed the patient's attack on the object.

Abraham (1912), in 'Notes on the psycho-analytical investigation and treatment of manic-depressive insanity and allied conditions', claimed that ambivalence between hate and love is much more radical in the depressed individual than in the obsessive neurotic individual. The melancholic, who feels hated because he projects his hatred outwards and perceives others as hostile, is unaware of his hatred and tends to think that people isolate him because of his illness.

For example, my patient constantly complained that her son and relatives did not care about her, but she was unaware of the fact that she did not take care of her son with due attention and affection to earn his gratitude.

A second paper by Abraham (1916) on melancholy looked at the depressed patient's orality, that is, his avidity, since the melancholic's peculiar character is his tendency to devour the love object.

In my patient's case, she had never been content with what the world offered her and in the transference would complain about what, in her eyes, represented my pleasure: my holidays or money.

Abraham (1916) stated:

> In his unconscious the melancholic depressed person directs upon his sexual object the wish to incorporate it. In the depth of his unconscious there is a tendency to devour and demolish his object. (p. 276)

This position generates a sense of guilt: if the melancholic aims to devour and envy, then his superego will tell him he is a greedy and negative person.

I believe that my patient had introjected a dismissive, depressed, and violent mother. Her father, by first and foremost supporting her qualities linked to success (intellectual) and beauty, had created a complex problem for her self-esteem, which was regulated solely according to her narcissistic functioning. If success was not achieved, the patient felt like a failure. The superego that supported her was in actual fact double-sided: her father would ask his daughter to be good at school to gratify himself before all else, and his daughter had introjected him as a narcissistic superego, ready to attack her if she did not operate at her best.

Lastly, it may be assumed that the patient, aside from her internal parents' requests, had developed a perception of failure in that she unconsciously 'knew' her success was down to acts of falsification and seduction. This is the blame and accusation that appears in the first dream.

Freud's contribution

Let us go back to Freud (1917e), who stated:

> Mourning is regularly the reaction to the loss of a loved person, or to the loss of some abstraction which has taken the place of one, such as one's country, liberty, an ideal… (p. 104)

In my patient's case, there might be mourning, given that she is about to lose her lover, a love object; but why then, instead of mourning, does she plunge into melancholy?

Freud said that there is no self-esteem disorder in mourning, which is a painful feeling that does not, however, lead to feeling impoverished. We know that the patient was aware of losing the love object, but the malaise was focused on herself, not on nostalgia for the lost love object. In this regard, Freud (1917e) stated:

> This indeed might be so even if the patient is aware of the loss which has given rise to his melancholia, but only in the sense that he knows *whom* he has lost but not *what* he has lost in him. This would suggest that melancholia is in some way related to an object-loss that is withdrawn from consciousness… (p. 106)

My patient knew she was not well because her lover had decided to leave her, but she did not know that the true, unconscious reason was that she had falsified her life and lost the good, constructive part of herself. The idea of winning back her lover would have been a defence enabling her to continue being a loved, admired, and seductive woman, pushing back her collapse. Since this defence could no longer be used due to the patient's mature age, her collapse could not be avoided.

Unlike mourning, where nothing regarding the loss is unconscious, in melancholy, one knows who is lost but not what is lost.

Freud (1917e) writes:

> In mourning it is the world which has become poor and empty; in melancholia it is the ego itself. The patient represents his ego to us as worthless, incapable of any achievement and morally despicable; he reproaches himself, vilifies himself and expects to be cast out and punished. He abases himself before everyone and commiserates with his own relatives for being connected with anyone so unworthy. He is not of the opinion that a change has taken place in him, but extends his self-criticism back over the past; he declares that he was never any better. This picture of a delusion of (mainly moral) inferiority is completed by sleeplessness and refusal to take nourishment, and—what is psychologically very remarkable—by an overcoming of the instinct which compels every living thing to cling to life. (p. 105)

And from here is the risk of suicide. He continues further on:

> He has lost his self-respect and he must have good reason for this. It is true that we are then faced with a contradiction that presents a problem which is hard to solve. The analogy with mourning led us to conclude that he had suffered a loss in regard to an object; what he tells us points to a loss in regard to his ego … If one listens patiently to a melancholic's many and various self-accusations, one cannot in the end avoid the impression that often the most violent of them are hardly at all applicable to the patient himself, but that with significant modifications they do fit someone else, someone whom the patient loves or has loved or should love. Every time one examines the facts this conjecture is confirmed. So we find the key to the clinical picture: we perceive that the self-reproaches are reproaches against a loved object which have been shifted away from it on to the patient's own ego. (p. 107)

Freud stated that the melancholic reproaches and torments his objects and himself. As I have shown in my clinical case, the analyst represents the tormented object but also the internal object that reproaches and torments the patient.

Ultimately, Freud said that self-accusations, clearly directed at the patient, are actually directed at the love object, so the apparent disaccord between the ego and the object is settled, as this same object has been introjected and is therefore placed in the patient's inner world. In another passage, despite not describing this mechanism of object introjection sufficiently clearly, Freud attributed it to infantile trauma.

Very concisely, Freud raised the issue of the original trauma:

> There is no difficulty in reconstructing this process. An object choice, an attachment of the libido to a particular person, had at one time existed; then, owing to a real slight or disappointment coming from this loved person, the object-relationship was shattered. (p. 108)

Originally, there was therefore a libidinal love investment in the mother and because of a real trauma, this investment was smashed.

According to Freud, the object fell inside the ego and the ego identified with the object, whereas in a normal process, the libido would have moved towards another object. 'Thus the shadow of the object fell upon the ego, and the latter could henceforth be judged by a special agency, as though it were an object, the forsaken object' (p. 108). Here Freud introduced the superego without defining it as such: in melancholy, aggressive identification with the traumatic object becomes part of the ego.

When the love relationship breaks, the child attacks the mother, the love object, and she responds by attacking him and reproaching him for being bad. The accusation and the attacking object will be interiorised in terms of an unhappy relationship in which the object and the subject will attack each other reciprocally: 'the shadow of the object fell upon the ego' and 'In this way an object-loss was transformed into an ego-loss and the conflict between the ego and the loved person into a cleavage between the critical activity of the ego and the ego as altered by identification' (p. 108). This is a highly concentrated sentence packed with suggestions: Freud was practically theorising the traumatic origin of a primitive superego.

The Freud–Abraham dialogue

When Freud sent his work on mourning and melancholy to Abraham before its publication, Abraham was perplexed: initially he did not understand why the melancholic patient identifies with the lost object, resulting in self-accusations also towards the object. Then, after having understood Freud's intuition that the melancholic, having lost the object, then aggressively reintrojects it, Abraham went further and asked himself why working through mourning can be done whereas working through melancholy is so difficult.

In melancholy, self-accusations directed at the love object prevent the love–hate conflict from being resolved, and aggressive hatred towards the lost object remains in the patient. For example, my patient was aggressive towards her husband and was unable to forgive his betrayal of her, despite the fact that she had betrayed him many times.

As for normal mourning, unlike Freud's understanding, according to which the libido invested in the lost object is gradually withdrawn from the object and then reinvested in another object, Abraham came to the conclusion that mourning is overcome during a long, complex process through which the subject constructs an introjected image of the loved person in his inner world. Loss concerns the disappearance of the real object, which stays alive, however, in the inner world. If it were not like this, and one just turned towards other love objects, it would be a maniacal defence against the loss.

Abraham identified working through mourning in a patient of his who, shortly after his wife's death, dreamt of being present at her post-mortem. The scene resembled animals that had been chopped up and displayed in a butcher's shop. At a certain point, the chopped-up parts came together, and the dead woman started to show signs of life. The patient clearly had an image of his wife as a fragmented and deteriorated object, but there was a reconstruction of the scattered fragments in his dream. According to Abraham, the dream was communicating the patient's successful working through of the mourning, the loved object no longer being lost because the patient had rearranged it so that it could be brought inside him, alive, never to be lost again.

Testimony to working through mourning can be found in a series of typical enough dreams in which the dead person appears as being alive; this means that the individual is working through the mourning, introjecting the lost loved one so that he may continue to live inside him.

Whereas Freud, in relation to mourning, underlined a gradual distancing of suffering under pressures from reality (the reality principle wins and the patient must acknowledge that the object has been lost), Abraham highlighted the importance of introjection and the reconstruction of the lost object as an internal object.

Here, in embryo, is the issue of gratitude and reparation. The fundamental difference between mourning and melancholy is that, unlike mourning, in the depressed patient, taking the object inside is more difficult because of a conflict of ambivalence; the depressed patient cannot separate from the object and remains joined to him through a bond of suffering he tortures with and is tortured by.

Abraham said that mourning needed time not so much because of libidinal clinginess to the lost object (as Freud had underlined), but because the inner object needed to be reconstructed and reanimated, given that it had been experienced as destroyed and in pieces.

In Abraham's more than in Freud's writings, the mother is also important as a source of trauma and suffering. Reading through Freud and Abraham's correspondence (Falzeder, 2002), it is clear how Abraham repeats that the melancholic's 'problem is with his mother', whereas Freud seems not to be listening. Disappointment and frustration at a time the mother is needed most coincide with oral sadism and lead to introjecting an object filled with hatred.

For Abraham (1924), the primitive trauma with the mother is reactualised in subsequent affective relationships. People who had early primary depression with their mother repeat the melancholic trauma each time they suffer affective trauma. Each new sentimental relationship connects back to the trauma and to the reactive hate of the first 'disappointment in love':

> The disappointment which the melancholiac has suffered as a child at the hands of his mother while he was still in a markedly ambivalent state of feeling has affected him in such a permanent way and made him so hostile to her that even his hatred and jealousy of his father has become of minor importance. (p. 460)
>
> If we want to realize the full strength of the melancholiac's hostility towards his mother and to understand the particular character of his castration complex ... we must keep in mind Starcke's theory that the withdrawal of the mother's breast is a 'primal castration'. (p. 463)

Abraham (1924) never mentioned primary destruction, as Klein instead did, but aggressive reaction to a trauma: 'Unable either to achieve a complete love or an unyielding hatred, he succumbed to a feeling of helplessness' (p. 469).

From the above, it is clear that Freud and Abraham described an object and a relational picture of melancholy that is still useful today. As I mentioned earlier, forms of depression are many and the analyst, also from a clinical and prognostic point of view, must be able to differentiate between them; with depressed patients in which there has certainly been infantile trauma, their history more than anything must be worked on, providing the patient with a type of relation that is different from that with the primary object, whereas with melancholic depression the approach must be different.

CHAPTER 16

Non-melancholic depression

To describe non-melancholic depression, I shall use clinical material of a female patient whose case I supervised.

Clinical case

The patient is a thirty-eight-year-old woman, unassuming and rather inexpressive, who dresses soberly. She expresses herself correctly but with a certain difficulty, as if she were not used to speaking about herself, expecting the other to do so for her. She speaks and is then silent, as if to invite questions that will let her continue to converse.

She complains of problems with romantic relationships. She left her partner, who is now with someone else. In the beginning she liked him, then she felt bored and decided to leave him. Her partner kept on insisting that they get back together but when she convinced herself to try again, he no longer wanted to. The patient tried to get back with him, insisting to the point of humiliating herself. Following this, she was unable to work; she stayed at home for two months and took psychotropic medication.

The patient went to a psychologist several times and was prescribed mental exercises, such as positive thinking: she thought these recommendations were useless. She did not, however, give up on the idea of needing someone, and, speaking to a friend, obtained the analyst's address.

My colleague arranged some initial consultations once a week to understand the patient's situation, but the patient said that once a week was not enough, considering her suffering and urgent need.

After several consultations and the analyst's suggestion to undergo analysis, the patient suggested a shorter therapy: she believed that a short but intensive therapy would bring her out of her crisis.

The patient lives alone, just a few kilometres away from her parents, whom she sees frequently; she has a dog that she leaves with them at weekends. She works in a bank, handling financing, and as she is very competent professionally, work is one of the things she cares about most.

She speaks about how she and her brother played happily together during childhood; and their father, too, when he came home, would join in. Their mother didn't know how to play; even today with her five-year-old grandson (the patient's brother's son), she just gives him paper to draw on and tells him where to draw the line. A picture of a mother unable to be in contact with the world of childhood emerges. During the patient's adolescence, her father stopped relating with her, he became isolated, and no longer contributed anything. Even today, according to the patient, he is quite absent, as if he lived at the bar and went home only at mealtimes. He drinks now and again, he is rather quiet, and his true companion is his dog. It became clear later on that the patient's mother had a marital crisis and left home to be with another man, but then went back. The mother, towards whom the patient is distant and feels ill-concealed irritation, is quiet and speaks only to criticise the patient's appearance: if she has brushed her hair, if she is well-dressed, or has eaten.

The patient likes travelling and going to bars with younger people, like her father. As for her romantic life, a constant relational pattern comes through: falling in love followed by increasing distance, and then boredom. Often, she is the one who leaves her partner and after a period of suffering, she looks for and finds a new love affair.

The patient mentioned attempting suicide at the age of eighteen, when she took psychotropic medication she had found at home; she was hospitalised but no one considered her action to be serious. When talking about this episode, it became even clearer how the patient would isolate her emotions, not connecting them up to her behaviour. At thirty-eight years of age, she had never thought about having a child, which was still a frozen vital project.

Her first dream: with some extra tipple in her bloodstream (the patient drinks occasionally), she dreamt she was in a coastal town, and wanted to move on to find a better beach. Perhaps she was in Morocco. She set off, and on her way found a nice beach where some people were in the sea; she wondered whether there were dangerous currents. She went to the beach and a lady of about sixty years old wanted to sell her some mineral water, which she did not buy as she noticed an automatic vending machine. The lady told her the machine was empty but the patient thought she was trying to cheat her, so she went to look for herself and found that it was indeed empty. So she decided to buy water from the lady after all.

She looked at the sea, which was that shade of green you only see in brochures. There were two tunnels on the sea, like train tunnels, one after the other, and they were half-filled with water. A boat went in, and she thought that there was a beautiful place on the other side. The patient associated this with hope: Morocco is not beautiful, but beyond the tunnels is Liguria... (from the patient's history we know that her grandfather, who was good to her, lived in Camogli in Liguria). She also associated it with Vietnam, which had been her favourite trip. Then she added that the lady in the dream could be her more approachable mother and the tunnels could be connected to her fear of the dark—shade then light.

Comment

This patient, apparently without emotions, was not cold, as she managed to arouse emotions in the therapist. Her way of communicating (speaking, then stopping and waiting for the analyst to complete the conversation) denoted a lack of an alive and articulate inner world that allowed her to feel in touch with others.

When a patient does not answer a question, or is embarrassed and talks about something else, it often means that he is unable to be in contact with his emotions. Therefore, during the evaluation period, keeping a silent listening position is not recommended; data needs to be gathered on the patient's past and present, starting, naturally, with what he brings to our attention, and then following intuitively the hypotheses that gradually form inside us.

For example, with this patient, it was very important to explore her past affective life, what was positive and what was deficient, and when and why she felt she was in a crisis (at the age of eighteen, she had no support and no life project). What I wish to highlight is that the first consultations need a target: we must have an idea of the areas we need to explore, gathering together the relational and emotional meanings that are deficient, since these are what will supply us with the right tools to work with.

We need to ask ourselves what experiences the patient has had: if he knows hate, love, gratitude. In the case I have described, we can see considerable diffidence towards the object that is depended upon, and therefore the therapist must provide an experience that helps gain motivated trust.

This person's main problem is that she did not know what her feelings were; she would go out with a man but did not know whether she loved him or not; she would leave him and then want to get back together with him. From the first consultation, it was possible to feel her uncertainty and confusion regarding her self.

Moreover, the clinical picture is one of a depressed and inhibited patient, regarding her emotional expression in particular; if it were depression similar to that of the previous case, her expressiveness would be much more explicit and dramatic, and her desperation would be communicated in words.

After separating from her partner, the patient started to feel lonely and anxious, she had no one and was suffering. If she were melancholic, she would have turned against her partner, but instead she just felt abandoned without attacking or accusing him. It could be argued that taking the initiative to leave her partner was aggressive, but the patient has neither a hard, disdainful character, nor did she leave him for another: she left him because she did not know whether or not she loved him. She appeared not to have narcissistic aspects, nor did she desire to take revenge on the object.

This patient fell into depression without any vindictive anger. If there was any anger, it remained as an unexpressed vital feeling. It does not seem as though she wanted to get back with her partner because she loved him, but in all likelihood because she was so distressed by the idea of being alone. This has nothing to do with the narcissistic attitude of the melancholic, who feels hurt and humiliated by being abandoned.

It is clear that the patient suffered from acute anxiety, from an inability to live alone, as if the object, by abandoning her, had taken away a vital part of her self. Perhaps this was her partner's function, and the patient had probably never really been in love with him. In fact, her anxiety tallies with a collapse of the self.

Whereas in the previous case the loss of the object was felt as an unbearable narcissistic wound, due to the patient's anger at being expelled by her husband and his lover, here the loss of the object brought with it an identity crisis and related unbearable anxiety. It was more a case not of the object but the self that was lost, having propped itself up by clinging to the object-partner.

Therefore, she declared that she needed therapy *immediately*: she could not bear the anxiety and one session per week was not enough. However, her perception of urgently needing therapy was not accompanied by an awareness of the trajectory that was needed to bring about change. She believed that once the anxiety symptom disappeared, everything would go back to the way it had been before.

In other words, the patient did not request that therapy bring about change. She merely wanted the therapist to help her make the anxiety symptom disappear. The patient felt like a foetus that had been expelled from the maternal womb (her partner's abandonment is tantamount to this), and needed the therapist to function as an accommodating womb. Therapy, however, is not only to protect this patient from anxiety but to help her build an identity.

The patient's existence mainly revolves around her job, meaning she has no adequate relational life. From what she has told the analyst, we know she has a dog, but her parents often look after it; this relationship with a dog can be a good sign that she wants an affective relationship, but we can also see a sign of a bond that arouses a certain claustrophobic anxiety, since the patient's parents are then entrusted with her dog.

Good parts, inviting the therapist to work with this patient, are visible. In the melancholic patient, these good aspects, despite being present, were blotted out by narcissistic anger that dominated her personality. This narcissistic anger did, however, represent a sign of vitality, whereas, in this patient, passivity and a lack of vital aggressiveness are predominant.

From her memories of the relationship with her parents, an affectionate, present father appears with her and her brother when they were young. It is likely, though, that this good experience was interrupted when the father and mother's relationship deteriorated. In any event, this father had been good at staying with his children when they were young but was then no longer present during their teenage years.

Moreover, it seems that the father had been a role model for her: she too became sullen and taciturn, had no real friends, and would stop for a drink at the bar, keeping company with people younger than her.

It is extremely important from the very beginning to try to have as much information as possible about the patient's history in order to reconstruct it. In this case, it is important to understand which parent the patient identified with, even regarding pathological aspects.

Another significant characteristic is the way in which this patient uses falling in love. She is often interested in men, goes out with them for a certain period, and then distances herself from them. Falling in love is a kind of pleasant mental state of euphoria used as an antidepressant, a way of reanimating dull vitality. The patient does not use objects narcissistically, a romantic relationship being a sort of pill for her pain and solitude.

The patient's mother, while expecting her second child, had entrusted the patient to her grandparents in Liguria from the age of eight to fifteen months. This patient does not have many memories of her childhood, her only memory being that of her father coming home from work and playing with her, and then taking her outside when it was dark to see the moon. Perhaps it is also this idyllic experience that she reproduces when falling in love.

The clog is the relationship with her mother, who went through a long period of depression and anger. The patient grew up in perennial sadness: she remembers throughout secondary school whole weekends spent in bed.

The melancholic patient from the previous chapter was in her prime during her adolescence: she was beautiful, an object of her father's admiration, and felt important to him, even though it was narcissistically. In this patient's case, however, there was an affective desert, except in childhood during those positive times with her father. Her depression is primary and continuous; even today, she suffers intensely because of a lack of meaning and support. Perhaps her attempted suicide in her youth was a way to put an end to unbearable pain that she was unable to share with anyone. Pain becomes unbearable if no one is willing to receive it, and her family was totally incapable of doing so. Even after being discharged from hospital, the meaning of her gesture failed to be understood.

I would like to return to the beach dream. The patient drank a little more than usual and dreamt of a beautiful beach, which she admired, even though she was convinced that there were more fascinating places. There were dangers (currents) and a suspicion that the woman offering her water wanted to con her. She checked the automatic vending machine but then just had to have trust. The vending machine seems to allude to her way of doing things alone without asking for help; only when it is empty (like now) is the patient obliged to accept help, even though she does not trust the woman (her mother and her therapist). The patient expressed in the dream what she was unable to say in words: that she is diffident and is afraid that the analyst has nothing to offer her but just wants to take her money away from her. The patient distrusts when she feels dependent, out of her fear of being deceived. The two tunnels invaded by water bring to mind depressive darkness and then maniacal illumination, but they are also signs of hope.

This first dream differs greatly from that of the melancholic patient. Here, there is no persecutory, narcissistic superego that shows the patient the flippancy of her existence (the church only had a façade). Instead, there is a vision of ideal happiness that attracts the patient. She moves from one place to another, but, afraid of the currents (we might think of emotional bonds), she does not stop. The dream also prefigures improvement that we may link to the 'journey' with the therapist, but it might also be travelling pleasure due to that 'one more glass', a sort of euphoric state that is not destined to last.

This 'one more glass' gives the patient the idea of a nice journey and an opportunity to reach a better beach: a sort of need to 'fill herself up' with something aesthetically rewarding.

It might be that the patient drinks to annul the action of a melancholic superego (as we know, the superego is soluble in alcohol), but here, unlike the previous patient, accusations towards the self are not evident, but some solitude anxiety is.

In this dream, depression is like a feeling of painful emptiness, and the defence is evasion (drinking to evade pain) and seeking ideal happiness.

This case differs immensely from the melancholic patient's defensive modes; through narcissistic pleasure and triumph, she had tried to escape from the truth about herself. In this case, however, the clinical problem is not so much narcissism, but no real identity because of the deficient environment the patient lived in. Fleeing from depressive anxiety occurs through mechanisms of evasion, like alcohol, falling in love and seeking out beautiful, fascinating places.

Klein (1963) wrote an excellent paper 'On the sense of loneliness', wherein she described distressing loneliness and compared it with being able to stay alone and feel creative.

In melancholic depression, as I sought to explain in the previous chapter, object relational theory as hypothesised by Freud, Abraham, and then Klein, is very useful clinically speaking.

Psychopathological pictures like this one are, however, better understood when Winnicott's theory of the self is referred to. In this case, therapy needs to be on a level that focuses on receptiveness and on stimulating the emotional potential of the self, given that we need to work with a defect or an arrest in potential development due to environmental shortcomings.

The patient requests nothing but relates with an automatic object (a vending machine) and has in mind an analysis that is separate from an affective dependent bond. In other words, she has developed defences against dependence and mechanisms that enable her to escape from psychic reality. The clinical problem is how she can be helped to structure dependence that is useful to her development.

This patient resorts to alcohol or falling in love to flee from suffering, but these defences, once their effect runs out, make her sink down into depression once more. Only an alive relationship with another significant human being will allow her to construct a vital inner world.

Affective deficiency

Tying in with infantile matters and the patient's affective deficiency, I would like to mention Spitz (1965), who examined the consequences of trauma and abandonment during early stages of life. His research involved children who, in some cases, let themselves die in an orphanage because of the loss of a love object, meaning that this syndrome resembles that resulting from the loss of the love object as described by Freud and Abraham.

Data that Spitz provided confirm that something happens extremely early on in traumatised patients that differs, however, from the melancholic situation, which concerns structures that are more mature and vitally aggressive.

Attacking the object (as can be seen in the first patient) is more vital than the withdrawal and emptiness in the second patient.

One may ask why this second type of patient is devitalised and so desolately passive. One possibility is that the patient perceives vitality as something dangerous, as a source of suffering, and therefore inhibits it, she annuls it. Areas of silent suffering, of unthinkable pain, are thus created, and treated by resorting to evasion, alcohol, or drugs.

In these traumatised patients, 'an attack on the libidinal self', as defined by Rosenfeld (1978), occurs. The child senses that the relationship, that is, dependence on a traumatising object, exposes him to terrible suffering; he therefore defends himself by inhibiting the vital and relational part of his self. The attack on the libidinal self, which has nothing to do with destructive narcissism, is an extreme form of defending oneself from trauma—a defence, however, that destroys development potentiality.

In the case of this depressed patient, we find ourselves facing a deficiency of affective or structuring responses. It seems that there was no emotional space in the mind of either parent for their daughter, they too living with pain. These are the situations that lead to *emotional development distortions*, which result in a pervasive feeling of non-existence.

To conclude, I would like to underline that, on the one hand, we have the Freud–Abraham–Klein model on depression, which can be applied to melancholic situations, and on the other, we have the Winnicottian model, that enables a better understanding of depression in traumatised patients who experience emptiness of the self.

Winnicott claimed that every human being is potentially able to develop should he find a facilitating environment: in analysis, the analyst must be this facilitating environment for the analysand.

Personal identity development underwent an arrest in the second patient, as she did not have emotionally present objects (a facilitating environment), such as a sufficiently intuitive mother or father regarding others' mental states and suffering. In these cases, not only the objects (the parents) are lost, but also important parts of the self and options for the future.

If we apply these reflections to our patient, we may say that she suffered a loss too early on, and, outside awareness, carries this pain of the loss of what she has never been able to live.

CHAPTER 17

Narcissism

Broadly dealt with in psychoanalytic literature is the complex concept of narcissism. As I have mentioned with regard to many other psychoanalytic terms, it bears several different meanings that range from being part of a normal personality to a pathogenic element that hinders development.

Narcissism officially entered psychoanalysis with Freud's essay 'On narcissism' (1914c). We know from Ernest Jones that Freud used the term narcissism for the first time at a meeting of the Vienna Psychoanalytic Society on 10 November 1909, where he said: 'Narcissism is a necessary half-way phase between auto-eroticism and alloeroticism' (p. 386). In Schreber's analysis (1911c), he stated:

> Recent investigations have directed our attention to a stage in the development of the libido which it passes through on the way from auto-eroticism to object-love. This stage has been given the name of narcissism ... This halfway phase between autoerotism and object love may perhaps be indispensable normally; but it appears that many people linger unusually long in this

condition, and that many of its features are carried over by them into the later stages of their development. (p. 386)

In his paper on narcissism, Freud (1914c) distinguished between 'ego-libido' and 'object-libido', and he also introduced the concept of the ego-ideal, which went on to develop into the superego. He considered narcissism both as a perversion and as a normal part of the egoism of self-preservation, and he saw it at work in megalomania and in withdrawal from the outer world in psychosis.

Freud was not, however, satisfied with this paper, as can be seen from a letter he wrote to Abraham. Moreover, he added further reflections in 'Mourning and melancholia' (1917e) and in Lesson XXVI of the *Introductory Lectures on Psycho-Analysis* (1916–1917).

This means that from the very start, this concept was difficult to frame because its parts were so complex that at times they seemed contradictory.

The following are several principal features of narcissism, according to Freud.

It is a healthy part of the libidinal drive of the survival instinct that belongs to every living creature.

It is found in the mental life of children and primitive peoples, where certain features bring to mind megalomania: the omnipotence of wishes and thoughts, magical beliefs in the power of words, and expectations about changing the external world via grandiose overtures.

Narcissism is also an aspect of pathology at an individual level. In schizophrenia, for instance, patients present with two basic characteristics: megalomania and withdrawing interest from the external world, from people and from things. This megalomania originates at the expense of object libido, which has been withdrawn from the outer world and directed onto the ego, at which point it transforms into pathological narcissism. The megalomania in itself is not a new creation here; on the contrary, it is an exaltation and clear manifestation of a condition that already existed previously.

In people whose libido suffered a setback, the object choice does not go towards the first love object, the mother, but oneself, which is clearly sought as the love object; these individuals exhibit a kind of object choice that must be defined as narcissistic.

On a concluding note, Freud believed that originally each human being has two love objects: himself, and his mother, who takes care of him. He thus assumed primary narcissism in everyone, and that in some cases it manifests predominantly. Narcissism is therefore an original disposition that can also explain the adult pathology. In this sense, Freud followed a parameter, which I have mentioned in previous chapters, according to which the *pathological* coincides with the *primitive*. So, the more the individual moves towards primary narcissism, the more he slides towards pathology.

The relationship between primitive and pathological led analysts to adopt different viewpoints on the positive or negative nature of narcissism. Considering a pathology as a developmental arrest sanitised the concept.

Indeed, some analysts consider narcissism as an infantile characteristic with developmental potential: among these are Balint, Kohut, and Winnicott. Others instead (particularly those from the Kleinian group) highlight the pathological side and conceive narcissism as a distortion, causing the individual to sacrifice dependence that fosters growth for the sake of grandiosity and a desire to control: narcissism, in their view, therefore impedes development.

These two ways of conceiving narcissism have never been conciliated. In a bid to simplify the issue, we may talk schematically of *benign narcissism* in identity defects, where immaturity and an arrest in emotional development are predominant, and destructive or *malignant narcissism* that predominates in the more severe pathologies.

Benign narcissism

A critique on Freud's conception of narcissism was written in 1960 by Michael Balint, who questioned primary narcissism, particularly the idea that severe patients, especially schizophrenics, could be considered as having regressed to primary narcissism. For Balint, these patients demonstrate relational complexity and not simply regression to a primitive stage. In Balint's opinion, the fixation point that regression moves towards in these cases is not necessarily primary narcissism, but a very primitive relational form. From the very beginning, the newborn primitively establishes a relationship with his family environment. If the care he receives is sufficient, he bonds with significant people in his environment, who then become his primary objects. Balint conceived this as *primary love*, a primitive relationship with the human environment that the child is surrounded by. He saw narcissism as secondary and forming in a harmonious fusion with the original objects. Frustration, which is inevitable in this kind of relationship, leads the infant to experience moments that differ from those harmonious exchanges between himself and the object, resulting in his withdrawing part of his investment from the environment and investing it in his developing ego.

One can feel a Winnicottian echo in Balint's words: this harmonious fusion with primary objects seems to allude to the infant–mother dual unit that is needed for development. Indeed, many years later, Winnicott (1971) turned Freudian theories upside down. Whereas Freud considered omnipotence as an illusory narcissistic function, Winnicott demonstrated that an early limitless illusory experience is not only necessary for growth but a basis for mental wellbeing.

When emphasis is placed on idealisation, one inevitably thinks of Kohut's (1971) relevant contribution. Both Kohut and Winnicott, despite their different theories and sources of inspiration, paved the way for new perspectives on the structural role of processes of idealisation in childhood. These two authors maintained that in an early stage of development children need to experience a positive illusion of omnipotence, and that through idealisation of the self and the object, a sense of individuality and personal meaning becomes structured.

Kohut (1966) stated that in psychoanalytic clinical work, there was a comprehensible tendency to consider narcissism as negative and that this prejudice was based on a comparison between narcissism and object love, the former being more primitive. The classical position on narcissism was, in his opinion, moralistic, as it set self-love against object-love, considering the former as negative. He, however, saw a 'double track': object libido and narcissistic libido, one leading to love towards the other and one leading to love towards the self.

A lack of adequate empathic responses in early stages of development leads to a lack of self-esteem. If a child suffers severe narcissistic traumas, he will end up with permanent personality damage, a narcissistic fixation, and a *grandiose self*, comprising exhibitionism and grandiosity, which will remain in its archaic form, generating pathology.

As can be seen, Kohut suggests a very open perspective on narcissism, and although in very different theoretical contexts, his perspective coincides with what Winnicott advanced as essential for a child's development. Winnicott too lent importance to the role of illusion (and infantile narcissism), that is, the child's belief that he has certain abilities he does not yet actually have, and he thought that the experience of illusion was essential in order to create a *potential space* for the self that the mother should not interfere with. By sustaining the illusion, the mother allows the child to experience objects that exist objectively but are created subjectively. This illusory dimension is fundamental to structuring the child's continuity of being.

As can be seen, these intuitions not only enable a better understanding of some stages of primitive development, but they also lead to changes in technique that, in the Kohutian school in particular, are based on using idealising aspects of narcissistic relations.

Negative narcissism

The Kleinian model on narcissism is very different from what has thus far been described. The main difference is that this model considers narcissism as a pathology linked to the death instinct.

Karl Abraham (1911) paved the way towards the clinical investigation of the narcissistic patient. In his opinion, when in analysis, these patients demonstrate uncommon diffidence towards the analyst; they often feel humiliated because of their narcissistic love for themselves, but they also feel superior to the analyst and seek to place him in an inferior position. Abraham (1919) connected this kind of transference to a conflict with an analyst seen as the envied father.

In the Kleinian group, Herbert Rosenfeld (1964), the most original and systematic scholar on this topic, thought that narcissistic object relations were a defence against acknowledging separation between the self and the object, which would result in inevitable frustration and envy. These patients' resistance derives from their superior attitude, which denies every kind of dependence. In severe narcissistic disorders, moreover, there is a rigid defence against all awareness of psychic reality. The clinical outcome of analysis is subject to the patient being able to establish a relationship of dependence with the analyst, which implies acknowledging separateness and difference, meaning moving towards what Klein called the depressive position.

Returning to Freud's theory on narcissism, according to which the libido is directed towards the self, Rosenfeld (1971) spoke of 'destructive narcissism', a structure expressing the death instinct, which attacks the healthy part of the self. He postulated that in severe psychopathologies an evil internal entity is idealised, a bad self, that distances the patient from contact with his emotions and relating with others. The idealised sick part gradually comes to dominate the rest of the personality by means of propaganda that promises easy solutions to all problems. This pathological structure resembles a delusional object that healthy parts of the personality tend to let themselves be captured by; pain disappears, and the subject is free to indulge in any kind of pleasant transgressive activity in fantasy. Destructive narcissism is organised like a criminal gang dominated by a leader who controls all its members, with the purpose of increasing their destructiveness.

Although the destructive part and the relational part may initially be balanced, the pathological part's goal is to dominate the whole personality. The destructive narcissistic structure can be represented by a grandiose figure who promises the patient wellbeing. This protection is, however, deceiving, and when the patient tries to flee from the control of the destructive narcissistic organisation, it threatens him with death, thus revealing its delinquent nature (Rosenfeld, 1971; Meltzer, 1973).

Rosenfeld, moreover, differentiated between two kinds of pathological narcissism: *libidinal* narcissism and *destructive* narcissism. Whereas destructive narcissism develops at the expense of the healthy part of the self, libidinal narcissism, based principally on self-idealisation, mainly occurs to the detriment of the object through excessive overestimation of the self.

In *Impasse and Interpretation*, Rosenfeld (1987) introduced a distinction between 'thin-skinned' and 'thick-skinned' narcissists. The former are hypersensitive, not dominated by destructive narcissism, and they develop narcissism due to humiliations suffered in early infancy; only secondarily do they then use it to triumph over their parents and the analyst. Thick-skinned narcissists have a psychopathological construction that is dominated by a sense of superiority and triumph.

Green (2002) too postulated a dual conception of narcissism: *positive* or *life* narcissism, whose purpose is directed at the perception of one's uniqueness, and *negative* or *death* narcissism, which tends towards level zero, and moves towards psychic death. This is not comparable to the usual distinction between healthy and pathological narcissism, given that even a slide towards positive narcissism is in any case pathological in that it impoverishes relations with objects. Nonetheless, it is less destructive than negative narcissism, which aims to impoverish the self, through to annihilating it. According to Green, some forms of depression that are principally based on asceticism and rejecting gratification are examples of negative narcissism.

Dominant in negative narcissism is the *disobjectalising* function, which annuls the *objectalising* function involved in addressing objects.

Considerations

At this point, several considerations may be made regarding the theoretical duplicity that accompanies the concept of narcissism.

On the one hand, 'good' narcissism is described (Balint, Kohut, Winnicott), an ideal condition of the self that needs to be empathically understood and reflected by parents for their child's realistic development, so that as far as possible, it can be free from sudden personality collapses.

On the other, 'negative' narcissism is described, in which the patient is tenaciously attached to his superior position, to his refusal to depend on anyone, to his sense of superiority, and to his disdain for others, leading him to pathogenic regression.

What differentiates the two models on narcissism whose visions are so different?

The first, which concerns development of the self, highlights environmental influences on the child's mind: the more empathic and sensitive the environmental response, the more harmonious his personality development.

The second model, which follows on from Freud's thought, sees the principal elements of its development in aggressive conflict and the strength of the drives. In this case, the conflict is not only with the love object, but it is also inner among the various parts of the personality, both sick and healthy. Here, the influence of the environment as well as traumatic events is of relative importance.

Each model follows its own vision of aggressiveness: it can be considered not as innate but a reaction to a negative environment, that is, a consequence of frustration and trauma; or it can be seen as part of an instinctive endowment of man, which also includes hatred and destructiveness.

It may also be said that the two types of narcissism refer to clinically different patients.

'Good' narcissism seems to originate in a mortifying environment that produced a series of permanent sufferings and caused a personality deficit. These individuals resemble those patients who are poorly individualised and have a weak personality, fearing their environment or passively adapting to it, that is, those which Rosenfeld defined as 'thin-skinned'.

The picture of patients that emerges from negative models of narcissism is instead much more varied and includes patients with destructive pathological structures.

One particular kind of narcissism is represented by forms of infantile withdrawal where psychotic development incubates. The patient lives in another reality and builds endless sensorial fantasies that he thinks are superior to psychic reality. This kind of narcissistic withdrawal brings to mind the mental state Freud described as a return to the intrauterine condition; it is, however, an active position of the patient's, where his construction of a delusional world that is felt as being superior fascinates him.

To conclude, I believe it can be said that there are many forms of narcissism, each of which must be considered in relation to the single patient. In some cases, we can find a narcissistic superego that pushes the patient to *perform* constantly, to then attack and denigrate him in moments of failure or crisis. In these cases, it is not the personality that is narcissistic but the superego that dominates the personality.

What can we say in the end about infantile narcissism?

Over recent decades, the conception of early child development has profoundly changed, particularly thanks to infant research (Sander, 1977; Stern, 1994; Beebe & Lachmann, 2002). We now have a picture of an interactive infant who relates immediately with his caregiver. This kind of research has disproved the pathologising vision of early analytic theories, which equated the primitive with the pathological, today it being anachronistic to speak of a child's primary narcissism. Nonetheless, children too become ill.

Why do some children choose to depend on a love object and develop an interest in life, while others build alternative worlds instead of human relationships? If depending on a protective object is good and useful, why should it be rejected? Why should a child be driven towards a narcissistic withdrawal and in so doing forgo relationships? It is highly likely that rejecting dependence and developing narcissistic structures depends first and foremost on a failed emotional relationship with the caregiver.

A narcissistic organisation can be a response to prolonged traumatic and deficient exposure, when the child is still very young and dependent, and his anxieties are too intense to permit alternative defences. This organisation develops in relational silence and creates a parallel narcissistic world that fascinates the patient and makes him feel superior.

At this point, we shall try to get to grips with the distinction between healthy narcissism and pathological narcissism. We have seen how self validation is important for mental growth. We can even say that although infantile idealisation of the self and objects is an illusion that derives from altering reality, it is necessary in order to keep the future alive; it should be distinguished from megalomaniacal fantasy, which impoverishes, since it falsifies and allows nothing to be constructed.

The benign or malignant nature of narcissism does not depend solely on idealisation in itself but on the quality of the object that is idealised. If something good is idealised, we move closer to infantile or libidinal narcissism (using Rosenfeld's words); should we idealise malice, control, and sadism, we move to the area of destructive narcissism.

I would like to conclude by reaffirming how important it is for the individual to feel that he is significant, and this is healthy narcissism. Eric Brenman (2006), who dedicated a great piece of work to the analyst's narcissism, stated: 'Where normal pride ends and omnipotence begins may be difficult to discern and, in my view, deprivation of the experience of being considered as significant is one element in intensifying omnipotence' (p. 25).

CHAPTER 18

Psychic withdrawal

The conceptualisation of this form of pathogenic structure allows us to distinguish between infantile play fantasies, which are part of the transitional and daydreaming area, and secret fantasies, which develop in a dissociated area of the mind and go on to construct an alternative reality that is extremely harmful to psychic and emotional development. There are various forms of withdrawal that can either be contained or develop over time.

Among the former kind of withdrawal, we find love and romantic fantasies that create a temporary idealised reality. A case similar to this is Carla's (Chapter 6): if she could, she would never have wanted her dreamed love to become real because this reality would have prevented her from staying in her fantasy withdrawal, a place of consolation that was always at her disposal so that she could escape reality. This form of circumscribed withdrawal is not particularly harmful because it does not lead to a significant alteration to reality perception, and even though it injures identity, omnipotence is not such that it will upset the mind. Because of her weak real identity, Carla was insecure, had panic attacks and needed the presence of a real partner to carry life forward.

In another female patient of mine, the juxtaposition of her real life and her life in a withdrawal provide a clearer contrast. In this case, too, the withdrawal was romantic. The patient would meet men once and verbally seduce them, then break off all contact, not even replying to phone calls if there were any. She would then enter a fantasy world with the man of the moment and try out every romantic experience with him. She carefully avoided all real encounters, as they would have discombobulated her fantasying pleasure, bar those times when she needed to see the man in flesh and blood because her memories were fading. A fine example in literature is *Oblomov* in Ivan Goncharov's novel, a character who spends his whole life indulging in fantasies for his future that he never makes for himself.

An increasingly common form of withdrawal today is that created by internet addiction. This kind of behaviour, when extensive, can turn into a mental withdrawal, that is, an invasive and repetitive experience in which virtual reality is considered more precious than relational life, because pleasure can be enjoyed in a sensory and illusorily rewarding parallel world.

Often withdrawals into the world of the internet begin in childhood via excessive addiction to video games (De Masi, 2009). In this case, we refer to *virtual reality*, a term with a contradictory ring to it: the noun *reality* is linked to certainty, to what is verifiable and exists, but its adjective *virtual*, to what is imaginary and hypothetical.

Virtual reality, however, is not only this. It often regards many of our shared beliefs. For example, how many of us do not know Santa Claus or Donald Duck? Both exist in an imaginary world, that is, in a virtual world. We would only be surprised if someone were to say that they met Donald Duck and had a chat with him. In this case, Donald Duck would cease to be that cute, mischievous character that metaphorically alludes to features found in each of us, and he would become a delusional perception. This example helps us understand how one can gradually pass from a withdrawal in which virtual reality is predominant to an experience that is delusional.

I have so far described some mental withdrawals that do not create major alterations to the perception of reality. The world of the withdrawal is parallel to reality and need not seriously interfere with it: a withdrawal of this type can be a defensive construction for underlying depression. During an analysis, we may similarly encounter a romantic transference, which is placed halfway between a dreamt event and a real fact, and it can remain for a long but limited period or transform into a delusional experience.

Other withdrawals are destined to create the premises for severe pathologies. In these cases, they cannot be defined as primitive defences, but *psychopathological constructions* proper. A psychopathological construction is more than just a primitive defence and it differs greatly: it is a new construction that has nothing to do with original development. It is often facilitated by emotional traumas and before long it starts to develop independently. Generally, it forms silently during childhood, and, over time, its pathogenic potentiality begins to be expressed. The distinction between defences and *psychopathological constructions or organisations* enables us to better identify those cases in which mental structures that maintain the illness but are difficult to pinpoint come into play. In short, we may say that whereas defences operate in the area of the neuroses, psychopathological constructions tend to lead the subject to the terrain of the psychoses.

Unlike defences, which do not completely destroy awareness, psychopathological constructions distort psychic reality until it does actually get destroyed. The patient, when he manages to leave this kind of mental state, is deeply distressed and depersonalised precisely because he no longer has the emotional perception that would enable him to understand psychic reality. Constructions like this are evident in the perversions as well as in borderline and psychotic conditions, where the patient can hypnotically regress towards a pleasant state of withdrawal that distances him from emotional reality.

I shall now look at the withdrawal as a specific pathological structure in severe patients, an extremely dangerous one at that, given that it tends to progressively colonise the healthy part of the personality.

John Steiner's book *Psychic Retreats* (1993) is a clear attempt to conceptualise this form of pathological organisation. Steiner conceives the retreat as a set of defence mechanisms and object relation systems that end up constituting a psychic place proper that the subject retreats to so that he can avoid unbearable emotions:

> The retreat then serves as an area of the mind where reality does not have to be faced, where phantasy and omnipotence can exist unchecked and where anything is permitted. This feature is often what makes the retreat so appealing… (p. 20)

Retreats, which defend the patient from paranoid–schizoid and depressive anxieties, can take on various aspects that range from living in a romantic fairy-tale world where everything is idealised, to a masturbatory withdrawal in pursuit of pornographic excitement; omnipotent fantasy, perverse relations, sadomasochism, and narcissism predominate in these retreats, all of which provide the self with a sense of pseudo-security and pseudo-protection. The main consequences of activating a pathological organisation, according to Steiner, are that object relations get distanced, and processes of psychic development are inhibited.

In analysis, the existence of a withdrawal can be seen from dreams in which violent and perverse addiction structures appear (ideological sects, totalitarian regimes, mafia-like or delinquent gangs), or uninhabited houses, caves, forts, or islands the subject withdraws to. At other times, as I illustrated in Carla's case (Chapter 6), the representation at the beginning of the dream is not terrifying but it then becomes so at the end.

The withdrawal can also maintain equilibrium at length in cases where there are no substantial psychopathological structures, but it usually tends to expand and subjugate the rest of the personality. This explains the pathogenic potentiality of some withdrawals that, having taken root in childhood, can result in psychosis in adulthood. Psychologically absent, parents often do not understand that their child is not simply good-natured and quiet, which in their eyes he seems to be, but that he has already withdrawn into an omnipotent world that is constructing his psychopathology. Since the withdrawal gradually alters contact with emotional reality and cancels the perception of abandonment and the parents' emotional absence, these children display no signs of their distress. At times, it may not even be a case of the parents being absent but anxious and intrusive, their interference bringing about the failure of an experience of good dependence. It is important to remember that, once set in motion, the process proceeds autonomously.

As I have already mentioned, the withdrawal is also, and first and foremost, a secret pleasant place where the patient creates his objects from scratch and loses himself in an exalting reality. Patients who are in analysis will usually be quiet about this for a long time, and only at a more advanced stage of their treatment will they communicate the existence of this secret place. Frequently, some obstinate moments of silence during therapy correspond to moments in which this secret space of the withdrawal is being nurtured.

As mentioned earlier, an excessive addiction to video games can at times be the starting point of psychic withdrawals that are destined to develop (De Masi, 2009).

Alberto, a six-year-old boy, was brought by his mother for a consultation, as she was worried about his excessive addiction to video games. Alberto's attraction to this world continued even after he had stopped playing. He identified with the characters in the video games and invented others himself. According to his mother, at times he would fall to the ground and 'play dead'. When he did this, he really did seem absent from the world, deriving enormous pleasure from this mental state and being so fascinated by it that he would repeat it over and over again. On one occasion, by taking advantage of his parents' lack of attention, engaged as they were in a garden party with friends, Alberto really did disappear. The adults looked for him in vain and then contacted the police. Alberto suddenly reappeared, not worried in the slightest, and was even amazed by his parents' concern; he had not thought about their being anxious and was amused by the thought of seeing them as they looked for him.

Withdrawing into the world of fantasy video games is more dominant in this child than his connection with reality; 'playing dead' or disappearing from his parents' sight for long periods is an exciting withdrawal exercise from the world. In mind are three other cases of adult psychotic patients who remembered how they would get excited as children by 'disappearing', which to them meant 'ending up in another world'.

Characteristic of these states is using perceptive organs to build artificial states of wellbeing, and employing the imagination to build virtual, parallel worlds. When these worlds appear in clinical material or dreams, it is important to describe them to the patient in detail, highlighting their pathogenic nature, since the patient mistakes what is pleasant for what is good and useful for his mind.

It is of utmost importance to understand that the psychic withdrawal of complex patients is not a static structure, but one that tends to develop and conquer the rest of the personality. In other words, it is an *intrapsychic delusional structure* that captures the healthy part and nourishes a gradual distortion of emotional reality.

My hypothesis is that the child who is destined to become psychotic has parents who not only do not know how to emotionally accommodate his projections, but also, at times, invade him with their own distressing experiences. In this case, the withdrawal is formed as a protective defence that tends to exclude the child from all contact with the relational world; it then becomes a forge that nourishes the psychotic part of the personality, which eventually ends up colonising the healthy part. The withdrawn child constructs a sensory parallel reality, another 'world' fed by imaginary fantasies that will accompany him until it brings into being a delusional experience.

The psychic withdrawal is a secret place that only the patient knows about. When speaking of a withdrawal's dissociated reality, the term dissociation does not refer to a vertical split in the personality, in which one part does not know what the other part is concealing, but to the fact that the world of the psychic withdrawal is nourished by fantasies that never encounter reality. To use an optical metaphor, it is as if the patient divided his vision in two: with one eye he can see the fantasy construction, and with the other reality. Given that these two visions never meet up, binocular vision can never be reached, and insight never produced. The two functions are kept separate, running in parallel without ever encountering one other. When the patient puts the dissociated fantasy world into operation, he closes off any access to reality perception. Yet another metaphor would be the mind working like a radio: when it is tuned into one radio station, it excludes all others.

I have sought here to show several forms of psychic withdrawal, from the mildest to the most dangerous, the latter tending to seriously distort the perception of reality. The withdrawal is not merely a place where one can stay to take refuge from anxiety, but it can become an alternative source of reality to the real world; it corresponds to the creation of a sensory reality that drains emotional development of lymph and closes off channels that useful experiences for mental growth could travel along. In particular, the withdrawal causes personal identity to deteriorate to varying degrees, both when it presents as a set of pleasant fantasies or daydreams, and when it is found in its most extreme forms as a dissociated psychotic world.

As mentioned earlier, the patient will seldom mention in analysis the existence of a withdrawal, any related fantasies, or the way in which he uses it; rather, he will defend and promote his secret, precious place. The analyst must therefore use his skill to identify a withdrawal in order to transform it into a shared experience, and at this point only can the analyst then begin to describe how it operates, what its purpose is and what effects it has on the patient's mind. Unfortunately, the patient, despite being conscious of having a secret life, is not aware of the destructive effects it has on his personality. Psychoanalytic work essentially consists in strengthening the patient's awareness by constantly describing the dynamics of the pathogenic part that draws him into the withdrawal, detaching him from relations and offering him false advantages of a life that is dissociated from reality.

My clinical experience has led me to think that intrapsychic interpretations which describe the dynamics between the contrasting parts of the personality are extremely useful in this case, in order to develop the patient's awareness of the withdrawal and the damage he inflicts on himself and on his ability to think. Transference interpretations to illustrate the patient's exclusion of the analyst from the relation are also important, but not as effective. I believe that the withdrawal should be treated as a drugging structure that tends to drain the individual of vitality, his emotional growth being sacrificed for the sake of the power of sensory pleasure.

I think that only in this way can a connection be established between the healthy part, which is always in danger of being weakened by the withdrawal's allure, and the analyst's work, whose purpose is that of helping the patient to make a distinction between what is pleasant but destructive and what is good and constructive.

CHAPTER 19

Final considerations

On a concluding note to this book, I would like to add a few points related to the subject of psychoanalytic therapy.

I shall not make reference to the numerous texts that have been written on this, such as that by Strachey (1934) on the effectiveness of transference interpretations and the way in which they should be communicated to the patient. I shall look instead at elements that allow the quality and the difficulty of this trajectory to be assessed.

In the past, certain criteria helped understand from the very start whether or not psychoanalysis was a suitable therapy for a particular individual; an established technique was used with the patient, who had to adapt to it and not vice versa. This theoretical framework did not take into consideration the fact that, at times, patients with worrying symptoms at the beginning were able to undertake a good journey, whereas others, who seemed to have all the qualities for a good analysis, could end up being much more difficult.

This practice of employing criteria of suitability for treatment has gradually gone out of use, even though clinical reality often tells us that there are cases which are difficult to treat. This is why it would be useful to reopen the debate on so-called 'difficult' patients.

In clinical reports today, the patient is often referred to non-specifically, and in some cases *the patient* is referred to without any details about his past, his suffering, or even his reasons for turning to analysis. At times, the material goes no further than a snapshot, disconnected from the entire therapeutic course, without even a slight reference to diagnostic criteria.

I do not believe that different patients with different pathologies can be treated in the same way according to an alleged single analytic method. Precisely for this reason, I insisted in the first chapters on needing to understand in depth the patient's psychopathological level, and to investigate his history, the quality of his internal objects, and his childhood experiences.

Let us look at what importance should be given to there being a psychic conflict or not. Usually, conflict directs us towards neurosis and not perversion, borderline pathologies, or psychotic disorders. In these last cases, psychopathological structures tend to conquer the healthy parts and colonisation occurs without there being any anxiety or apparent conflicts.

This is why neurotic situations better suit psychoanalytic therapy. Despite the limits and suffering that accompany the neurotic patient, potentially he has the cognitive and emotional tools to understand why he is suffering and how he can transform it. Being able to understand dreams, which neurotic patients often can, is extremely important so that the level of intuitive ability can be raised. Using intuition to understand the reasons behind these patients' malaise certainly does not put an end to their suffering but it does permit it to be contained through understanding.

Recovering perceptive and emotional functions in neurotic patients is done by recovering the self's repressed or projected parts, given that one mechanism of the neurotic structure operates according to repression or projection. Repression is less damaging than projection, as it is a dynamic process in which the repressed content remains in connection with consciousness; repressed thoughts are likely to appear in dreams and be recovered by the dreamer.

Projection is a more complex mechanism since a part of the self is alienated and the subject tends to become impoverished; this is more frequent in narcissistic personalities, which, in order to believe they are superior, project what is unpleasant onto others. In other patients, however, it is the good parts that are projected and not recognised as one's own.

Yet another component of neurotic suffering derives from the pathogenic action of the superego. There are individuals who arrive in analysis with deep self-disparagement because they are dominated by a voice that distorts each and every positive thought they have. A superego's perverse distortion is extremely structured, and in some cases can take a very long time to be transformed.

In melancholic depression, there is a manic-depressive oscillation in which moments of narcissistic exaltation are followed by moments of self-accusation and aggressive attacks.

Instead, in cases in which patients have poor self-esteem, the superego mortifies and destroys any acknowledgement or gratification. If a patient, for example, believes he has done something good, he is suddenly accused of pathological narcissism, greed, and egocentrism. In these cases, the superego is a perverse entity against life and development. Frequently, it is discovered that this structure derives from repeated traumas often inflicted by the parents, by depressed mothers, for instance, who denied their child's personality of any worth.

In these cases, the analyst must pay particular attention to how his interventions are received, especially those that are negative. In fact, in many cases the patient's superego is ready to translate them into accusations. For this reason, it is always important to listen carefully to the patient's response to the interpretation that is offered.

Other types of neurotic patient are those who suffer from phobias or panic attacks. This kind of patient often suspends therapy as soon as the symptom disappears, meaning that he was not looking for real transformation but just hoping that the symptom could ease or disappear altogether.

Thus far, I have mentioned rather common neurotic manifestations in psychoanalytic practice; these are situations that until a certain point allowed life to be lived bearably, but then defences collapsed because a trauma or emotional loss occurred, or growing older set in.

Suffering connected to growing old is rather neglected by psychoanalytic literature. Besides midlife crises, profound distress can also accompany an elderly person, who must cope with his body becoming weaker and deteriorating, the loss of his same-generation friends, loneliness, and the prospect of death. Cases treated analytically that are found in the literature have surprisingly good results. It would therefore be very useful if analysts were more aware of the elderly person's request for help, considering that these individuals often have no objects that can accommodate their anxiety and transform it.

With other patients, the analytic course is much more complex, and, at times, we must realise that it is impossible to proceed beyond a certain limit. These are not impasses, which I described earlier on, but conditions that cannot be transformed, that is, those psychopathological structures which interfere with being able to use emotional-intuitive thought.

An example would be that of a patient who is colonised by a sexualised withdrawal that removes him from the analytic relationship and attempts to transform the analyst into a depressed and eroticised being, just like his mother, thus blocking any chance of a relationship that is useful to psychic development.

Once a patient like this dreamt that he was in a deep valley where there was a horse race but no track and no reins. Suddenly, the patient realised that there was a figure coming towards him. With some effort, he managed to make out that it was a pig—he was astonished. What was a pig doing there? The animal's expression was so wise and sad that he could not take his eyes off it.

The patient associated the pig with a representation of himself; the wild unbridled horses were his excited and uncontained sick parts. The pig that looked at him sadly was depression underlying his transgressive and sexualised state.

This clinical material is testimony to how the pathological structure continues to conquer the patient's mind even during his analysis. The sexualised part, which is fascinating, is a constant factor in perversion, and the analyst must repeatedly describe it and stress the ease with which it conquers mental space. This patient, facilitated by his mother's eroticised attention, had developed an early sexualised withdrawal which drove him to early pathological development. In this case, as I mentioned earlier, intrapsychic interpretations are extremely useful, as they clarify the inner struggle between the sick and the healthy parts. Should this kind of intervention not occur, the risk is that the sick part will colonise the healthy part. Only by containing the power of the perverse part can the patient be helped to develop a true identity.

Psychoanalytic therapy avails itself of a natural function of the mind—*emotional-intuitive functioning*—which allows one's mental processes to be observed; this is unconscious functioning potentially present in each of us, bar those patients we are now considering.

In these patients' therapy, we find ourselves on particular terrain, as the processes that enable the development of symbolisation and emotional containment are deficient here. In other words, the unconscious, as we are used to it being represented, is not operative, and awareness is lacking. Consequently, the analyst must work in difficult conditions, and he will often lose contact with the patient. Interpretations are not understood, or they are often forgotten because introjective processes and associative thought, which would permit an intuitive understanding of psychic facts, are lacking; moreover, there being no free associations also affects those dreams that seem clear to the analyst but have no meaning for the dreamer.

Also in the case of patients heading towards psychosis is the intuitive thought function severely deficient; since childhood, these individuals have lived in a withdrawal that is dissociated from reality, a secret world where they construct the psychosis. The delusion, too, in its manifest or cryptic forms, is a sensory construction that takes the place of thought.

These considerations are my attempt to understand the complexity of therapy for the increasing number of non-neurotic patients. These are extremely difficult patients to reach: some cannot respect the formal setting, arriving late for their sessions, being unable to organise their time, and presenting problems such as not even remembering what happened during important moments of the treatment. In particular, they cannot adapt to the implicit conditions of analysis that bases its functioning on receptive readiness in the individual undergoing therapy. None of this should discourage the analyst but stimulate him to find new channels of communication with the patient. And this occurs with greater ease when working with those patients who have blocked but not destroyed their development potentiality and are unscathed by considerable psychopathological constructions that have colonised the mind.

Investigating mysterious functions of the mind and the complex reasons that produce them is what the analyst's real creativity consists in. Growth of the mind can occur only in an encounter with an analytic mind that functions as a new object.

References

Abraham, K. (1907). On the significance of sexual trauma in childhood for the symptomatology of dementia praecox. In: *Clinical Papers and Essays on Psychoanalysis*. London: Hogarth, 1955.

Abraham, K. (1911). Giovanni Segantini: a psycho-analytical study. In: *Clinical Papers and Essays on Psychoanalysis*. London: Hogarth, 1955.

Abraham, K. (1912). Notes on the psycho-analytical investigation and treatment of manic-depressive insanity and allied conditions. In: *Selected Papers on Psychoanalysis*. London: Hogarth, 1927.

Abraham, K. (1916). The first pregenital stage of the libido. In: *Selected Papers on Psychoanalysis*. London: Hogarth, 1927.

Abraham, K. (1919). A particular form of neurotic resistance against the psycho-analytic method. In: *Selected Papers on Psychoanalysis*. London: Hogarth, 1927.

Abraham, K. (1924). A short study of the development of the libido, viewed in the light of mental disorders. In: *Selected Papers on Psychoanalysis*. London: Hogarth, 1927.

Abram, J. (2002). *The Language of Winnicott: A Dictionary of Winnicott's Use of Words*. New York: Routledge, 2008.

Ainsworth, M., Blehar, M., Waters, E., & Wall, S. (1978). *Patterns of Attachment*. Hillsdale, NJ: Erlbaum.

Balint, M. (1960). Primary narcissism and primary love. *Psychoanalytic Quarterly, 29*: 6–43.

Balint, M. (1968). *The Basic Fault: Therapeutic Aspects of Regression*. Evanston, IL: Northwestern University Press.

Baron-Cohen, S. (1987). Autism and symbolic play. *British Journal of Developmental Psychology, 5*: 138–149.

Beebe, B., & Lachmann, F. M. (2002). *Infant Research and Adult Treatment: Co-constructing Interactions*. Hillsdale, NJ: The Analytic Press.

Beebe, B., Lachmann, F. M., & Jaffe, J. (1997). Mother–infant interaction structures and presymbolic self- and object representations. *Psychoanalytic Dialogues, 7*: 133–182.

Bezoari, M. (2002). La nevrosi di transfert come funzione del campo analitico (Transference neurosis as a function of the analytic field). *Rivista di Psicoanalisi, 48*: 889–905.

Bick, E. (1968). The experience of the skin in the early object relation. *International Journal of Psychoanalysis, 49*: 484–486.

Bion, W. R. (1965). *Transformations: Change from Learning to Growth*. London: Heinemann.

Bion, W. R. (1967). *Second Thoughts: Selected Papers in Psycho-Analysis*. London: Heinemann.

Bion, W. R. (1992). *Cogitations*. Edited by F. Bion. London: Karnac.

Bollas, C. (1979). The transformational object. *International Journal of Psychoanalysis, 60*: 97–107.

Bollas, C. (1987). *The Shadow of the Object. Psychoanalysis of the Unthought Known*. New York: Columbia University Press.

Bollas, C. (1992). *Being a Character: Psychoanalysis and Self Experience*. New York: Hill & Wang.

Bordi, S. (2004). Foreword to *Making Death Thinkable* by Franco De Masi (pp. 13–20). London: Free Association Books.

Bowlby, J. (1980). *Attachment and Loss*. Vol. III. London: Hogarth.

Brenman, E. (2006). *Recovery of the Lost Good Object*. New York: Routledge.

Craparo, G. Ortu, F., & Van der Hart, O. (Eds.) (2019). *Rediscovering Pierre Janet: Trauma, Dissociation and a New Context for Psychoanalysis*. Abingdon, UK: Routledge.

Damasio, A. (2010). *Self Comes to Mind: Constructing the Conscious Brain*. New York: Pantheon.

Davies, J. T. (1996). Dissociation, repression, and reality testing in the countertransference: the controversy over memory and false memory in the psychoanalytic treatment of adult survivors of childhood sexual abuse. *Psychoanalytic Dialogues, 6*: 189–218.

Davies, J. T. (2001). Revisiting psychoanalytic interpretation of the past: an examination of declarative and non-declarative memory processes. *International Journal of Psychoanalysis, 82*: 449–461.

De Masi, F. (2006). *Making Death Thinkable*. London: Free Association.

De Masi, F. (2009). *Vulnerability to Psychosis: A Psychoanalytic Study of the Nature and Therapy of the Psychotic State*. London: Karnac.

Deutsch, H. (1955). The impostor: contribution to ego psychology of a type of psychopath. *Psychoanalytic Quarterly, 24*: 483–505.

Di Chiara, G. (1985). Una prospettiva psicoanalitica del dopo Freud: un posto per l'altro. *Rivista di Psicoanalisi, 31*: 451–461.

Edelman, G. M. (1992). *Bright Air, Brilliant Fire: On the Matter of the Mind*. New York: Basic Books.

Falzeder, E. (Ed.) (2002). *The Complete Correspondence of Sigmund Freud and Karl Abraham 1907–1925*. London & New York: Routledge, 2018.

Ferenczi, S. (1919). *Further Contributions to the Theory and Technique of Psycho-Analysis*. London: Hogarth, 1955.

Fonagy, P. (1999). Memory and therapeutic action. *International Journal of Psychoanalysis, 80*: 215–223.

Fonagy, P., Target, M., Gergely, G., Allen, J. G., & Bateman, A. W. (2003). The developmental roots of borderline personality disorder in early attachment relationships: a theory and some evidence. *Psychoanalytic Inquiry, 23*: 412–459.

Fornari, F. (1966). Nota sul rapporto d'oggetto adolescenziale. *Rivista di Psicoanalisi, 12*: 49–59.

Fosshage, J. L. (1994). Toward reconceptualising transference: theoretical and clinical considerations. *International Journal of Psychoanalysis, 75(2)*: 265–280.

Freud, S. (1894a). *The neuro-psychoses of defence*. S. E., 3: 41–61.

Freud, S. (1895b). On the grounds for detaching a particular syndrome from neurasthenia under the description 'anxiety neurosis'. S. E., 3: 90–115.

Freud, S. (1895c). *Obsessions and phobias*. S. E., 3: 74–82.

Freud, S. (1895d). *Studies on Hysteria* [with J. Breuer]. S. E., 2: 19–305.

Freud, S. (1905e). *Fragment of an Analysis of a Case of Hysteria*. S. E., 7: 1–122.

Freud, S. (1905d). *Three Essays on the Theory of Sexuality*. S. E., 7: 125–245.

Freud, S. (1909b). *Analysis of a Phobia in a Five-Year-Old Boy. S. E.*, 10: 1–150.
Freud, S. (1911c). *Psychoanalytic Notes upon an Autobiographical Account of a Case of Paranoia (Dementia Paranoides). S. E.*, 12: 3–82.
Freud, S. (1912b). The dynamics of transference. *S. E.*, 12: 99–108.
Freud, S. (1914c). On narcissism: an introduction. *S. E.*, 14: 67–102.
Freud, S. (1915e). The unconscious. *S. E.*, 14: 159–215.
Freud, S. (1916–1917). *Introductory Lectures on Psycho-Analysis. S. E.*, 15–16: 243–463.
Freud, S. (1917e). Mourning and melancholia. *S. E.*, 14: 237–258.
Freud, S. (1918b). *From the History of an Infantile Neurosis. S. E.*, 17: 7–122.
Freud, S. (1920g). *Beyond the Pleasure Principle. S. E.*, 18: 7–64.
Freud, S. (1923b). *The Ego and the Id. S. E.*, 19: 3–66.
Freud, S. (1926d). *Inhibitions, Symptoms and Anxiety. S. E.*, 20: 77–174.
Freud, S. (1930a). *Civilization and its Discontents. S. E.*, 21: 59–145.
Glover, E. (1927). Lectures on technique in psychoanalysis. *International Journal of Psychoanalysis*, 8: 311–338.
Goncharov, I. (1859). *Oblomov*. London: Alma, 2014.
Green, A. (1980). The dead mother. In: *On Private Madness*. London: Hogarth, 1986.
Green, A. (2001). *Life Narcissism, Death Narcissism*. London: Free Association.
Green, A. (2002). A dual conception of narcissism: positive and negative organizations. *Psychoanalytic Quarterly*, 71: 631–649.
Greenson, R. R. (1965). The working alliance and the transference neurosis. *Psychoanalytic Quarterly*, 34: 155–181.
Grossman, V. (2013). *An Armenian Sketchbook*. London: MacLehose.
Grotstein, J. S. (1981). *Do I Dare Disturb the Universe? A Memorial to Wilfred R. Bion*. Beverly Hills: Caesura.
Gusnard, D. A., Akbudak, E., Shulman, G. L., & Raichle, M. E. (2001). Medial prefrontal cortex and self-referential mental activity. *Proceedings of the National Academy of Sciences of the USA*, 98: 4259–4264.
Hartmann, H. (1964). Concept formation in psychoanalysis. *The Psychoanalytic Study of the Child*, 19: 11–47.
Heimann, P. (1950). On countertransference. *International Journal of Psychoanalysis*, 31: 81–84.
Heimann, P. & Isaacs, S. (1952). Regression. In: M. Klein, P. Heimann, S. Isaacs, & J. Riviere (Eds.), *Developments in Psycho-Analysis*. London: Hogarth.

Inderbitzin, L. B. & Levy, S. T. (2000). Regression and psychoanalytic technique: the concretization of a concept. *Psychoanalytic Quarterly, 69*: 195–223.

Jackson, S. W. (1969). The history of Freud's concept of regression. *Journal of the American Psychoanalytic Association, 17*: 743–784.

Jaques, E. (1965). Death and the mid-life crisis. *International Journal of Psychoanalysis, 46*: 502–514.

Johnson, M. K., Raye, C. L., Mitchell, K. J., Touryan, S. R., Greene, E. J., & Nolen-Hoeksema, S. (2006). Dissociating medial frontal and posterior cingulate activity during self-reflection. *Social Cognitive and Affective Neuroscience, 1*: 56–64.

Joseph, B. (1985). Transference: the total situation. *International Journal of Psychoanalysis, 66*: 447–454.

Khan, M. R. (1963). The concept of cumulative trauma. *The Psychoanalytic Study of the Child, 18*: 286–306.

Klein, M. (1946). Notes on some schizoid mechanisms. *International Journal of Psychoanalysis, 27*: 99–110.

Klein, M. (1948). A contribution to the theory of anxiety and guilt. *International Journal of Psychoanalysis, 29*: 113–123.

Klein, M. (1952). The origins of transference. *International Journal of Psychoanalysis, 33*: 433–438.

Klein, M. (1963). On the sense of loneliness. In: *Envy and Gratitude and Other Works 1946–1963*. London: Hogarth, 1975.

Kohut, H. (1966). Forms and transformation of narcissism. *Journal of the American Psychoanalytic Association, 14*: 243–272.

Kohut, H. (1971). *The Analysis of the Self: A Systematic Approach to the Psychoanalytic Treatment of Narcissistic Personality Disorders*. Chicago: University of Chicago Press, 2009.

Kris, E. (1952). *Psychoanalytic Explorations in Art*. Madison, CT: International Universities Press.

LeDoux, J. (1996). *The Emotional Brain: The Mysterious Underpinnings of Emotional Life*. New York: Simon & Schuster.

Levin, F. M. (2009). *Emotion and the Psychodynamics of the Cerebellum*. London: Karnac.

Lou, H. C., Luber, B., Crupain, M., Keenan, J. P., Nowak, M., Kajer, T. W., Sakeim, M. A., & Lisanby, S. H. (2004). Parietal cortex and representation of the mental self. *Proceedings of the National Academy of Sciences of the USA, 101*: 6827–6832.

Mancia, M. (2004). *Sentire le parole. Archivi sonori della memoria implicita e musicalità del transfert.* Torino: Bollati Boringhieri.

Meltzer, D. (1966). The relation of anal masturbation to projective identification. *International Journal of Psychoanalysis, 47*(2): 335–342.

Meltzer, D. (1973). *Sexual States of Mind.* London: Karnac.

Miller, F. & Bashkin, E. A. (1974). Depersonalization and self-mutilation. *Psychoanalytic Quarterly, 43*: 638–649.

Modell, A. H. (1999). The dead mother syndrome and the reconstruction of trauma. In: G. Kohon (Ed.), *The Dead Mother: The Work of André Green* (pp. 76–86). London: Routledge.

Momigliano, L. N. (1987). A spell in Vienna—but was Freud a Freudian?—an investigation into Freud's technique between 1920 and 1938, based on the published testimony of former analysands. *International Review of Psychoanalysis, 14*: 373–389.

Money-Kyrle, R. (1956). Normal counter-transference and some of its deviations. *International Journal of Psychoanalysis, 37*: 360–366.

Money-Kyrle, R. (1971). The aim of psychoanalysis. *International Journal of Psychoanalysis, 52*: 103–106.

Northoff, G., Heinzel, A., de Greck, M., Bermpohl, F., Dobrowonly, H., & Panksepp, J. (2006). Self-referential processing in our brain: a meta-analysis of imaging studies on the self. *Neuroimage, 31*(1): 440–457.

Ogden, T. H. (1994). *Reverie and Interpretation.* Lanham, MD: Jason Aronson.

Orange, D. M. (1998). *Emotional Understanding.* New York: Guilford.

Pick, I. B. (1985). Working through in the countertransference. *International Journal of Psychoanalysis, 66*: 157–166.

Putnam, F. W. (1997). *Dissociation in Children and Adolescents: A Developmental Perspective.* New York: Guilford.

Racker, H. (1953). A contribution to the problem of counter-transference. *International Journal of Psychoanalysis, 34*: 313–324.

Racker, H. (1957). The meaning and uses of countertransference. *Psychoanalytic Quarterly, 26*: 303–357.

Renik, O. (1998). The analyst's subjectivity and the analyst's objectivity. *International Journal of Psychoanalysis, 79*: 487–497.

Rosenfeld, H. (1964). On the psychopathology of narcissism: a clinical approach. *International Journal of Psychoanalysis, 45*: 332–337.

Rosenfeld, H. (1971). A clinical approach to the psychoanalytic theory of life and death instincts: an investigation into aggressive aspects of narcissism. *International Journal of Psychoanalysis*, 52: 169–177.

Rosenfeld, H. (1978). Notes on the psychopathology and psychoanalytic treatment of some borderline patients. *International Journal of Psychoanalysis*, 58: 215–239.

Rosenfeld, H. (1987). *Impasse and Interpretation*. London: Tavistock.

Sander, L. W. (1977). The regulation of exchange in infant–caregiver systems and some aspects of the context–contrast relationship. In: L. A. Rosenblum (Ed.), *Interaction, Conversation and the Development of Language*. New York: Wiley.

Sandler, J. & Sandler, A.-M. (1984). Theoretical and technical comments on regression and anti-regression. *International Journal of Psychoanalysis*, 75: 431–439.

Sandler, J. & Sandler, A.-M. (1987). The past unconscious, the present unconscious and the vicissitudes of guilt. *International Journal of Psychoanalysis*, 68: 331–441.

Schafer, R. (1983). *The Analytic Attitude*. New York: Routledge.

Segal, H. (1954). A note on schizoid mechanisms underlying phobia formation. *International Journal of Psychoanalysis*, 35: 238–241.

Spence, D. P. (1982). *Narrative Truth and Historical Truth: Meaning and Interpretation in Psychoanalysis*. New York: W. W. Norton, 1984.

Spillius, E. B. (2007). *Encounters with Melanie Klein*. London: Routledge.

Spillius, E. B., Milton, J., Garvey, P., Couve, C., & Steiner, D. (2011). *The New Dictionary of Kleinian Thought*. London: Routledge.

Spitz, R. (1965). *First Year of Life: A Psychoanalytic Study of Normal and Deviant Development of Object Relations*. Madison, CT: International Universities Press.

Steiner, J. (1993). *Psychic Retreats: Pathological Organisations of the Personality in Psychotic, Neurotic, and Borderline Patients*. London: Routledge.

Stern, A. (1924). On the counter-transference in psychoanalysis. *Psychoanalytic Review*, 11: 166–174.

Stern, D. N. (1994). One way to build a clinically relevant baby. *Infant Mental Health Journal*, 15: 9–25.

Stolorow, R. D. & Atwood, G. E. (1992). *Contexts of Being: The Intersubjective Foundations of Psychological Life*. Hillsdale, NJ: The Analytic Press.

Stolorow, R. D., Atwood, G. E., & Brandchaft, B. (1994). *The Intersubjective Perspective*. Lanham, MD: Jason Aronson.

Strachey, J. (1934). The nature of the therapeutic action of psychoanalysis. *International Journal of Psychoanalysis, 15*: 127–159.

Tronick, E. (1989). Emotions and emotional communication in infants. *American Psychologist, 44*(2): 112–119.

Williams, P. (2004). Incorporation of an invasive object. *International Journal of Psychoanalysis, 85*: 1333–1348.

Winnicott, D. W. (1954). Metapsychological and clinical aspects of regression within the psychoanalytical set-up. *International Journal of Psychoanalysis, 36*: 16–26.

Winnicott, D. W. (1965). *The Family and Individual Development*. London: Tavistock.

Winnicott, D. W. (1971). *Playing and Reality*. London: Tavistock.

Zimmer, C. (2005). The neurobiology of the self. *Scientific American, 293*(5): 92–96.

Index

Abraham, K., 20, 22, 58, 93, 129
    Freud–, 117–119
    melancholic depression, 113–114
    melancholy, 113
    narcissism, 135
Abram, J., 62
actual neuroses, 19, 66, 77 *see also* anxiety
Ainsworth, M., 71
Allen, J. G., 98
analytic relationship, 2, 18, 37, 39–41
anxiety, 20, 65, 66, 68, 69–72
    attachment theory, 70–71
    automatic, 72
    castration, 66
    clinical work, 73–74
    cumulative trauma, 71
    death instinct, 69
    defence, 67
    depersonalising, 107
    depressive, 68, 128
    dissociation, 72
    hysterical, 86
    internal conflict patterns, 66–67
    Klein, Melanie, 68–69
    panic attack, 74
    posttraumatic, 87
    protective shield, 67, 70, 71, 88
    signal, 68, 72
    traumatic, 72–73, 92
attachment theory, 23, 70–71, 94–95
Atwood, G. E., 23, 27

Balint, M., 60, 89, 133, 137
Baron-Cohen, S., 99
Bashkin, E. A., 103
Bateman, A. W., 98
Beebe, B., 13, 15, 98, 138
Bezoari, M., 38
Bick, E., 81
Bionian theory, 22
Bion, W. R., 26–27, 50, 53, 70, 89, 106–107
    -K, 28, 35
    reverie, 52
    theory, 22
    transference, 38

Bollas, C., 27, 41, 90
Bordi, S., 71
Bowlby, J., 70
Brandchaft, B., 23
Brenman, E., 11, 44, 139
Breuer, J., 87

cognitive science, 1
cognitive therapy, 84
consciousness, 24, 40, 98, 99 *see also* unconscious
    unconscious and, 87
    higher-order, 100–101
    primary, 100, 101
container, 22, 50, 70, 94
countertransference, 47, 51, 53–55
    see also transference
    analyst, 48–49
    concept, 48–50
    Ogden, 52–53
    projective identifications, 49–50
    as reverie, 52–53
    unconscious bases of, 50–52
Craparo, G., 87, 91

Damasio, A., 99
Davies, J. T., 72, 91
Dead Mother, The, 93
death instinct, 69
De Masi, F., 142, 145
depersonalisation
    anxiety, 107
    borderline, 103–104, 107
    differentiating neurotic and psychotic, 107
    neurotic, 102, 107
    psychotic, 104–105, 105–107
depression, 109, 119, 130, 137, 143, 151
destructiveness, 21, 74, 136, 138
Deutsch, H., 48, 107
Di Chiara, G., 41
dissociation, 72, 91, 92, 94, 146–147
    see also anxiety; psychic withdrawal
dreams, 18, 26–27, 31, 35–36, 52, 53, 58, 83, 90, 92, 95, 144, 150, 153
    impasse in, 45–46
    mourning and, 118

Edelman, G. M., 100

false self, 107
Falzeder, E., 119
fear 78–79
Ferenczi, S., 48, 89
Ferro, A., 52
Fonagy, P., 90, 98
Fornari, F., 101
Fosshage, J. L., 39
Freud, S., 2, 25–26, 74, 129
    –Abraham, 117–119
    analyst and patient relationship, 48
    anxiety, 65–68
    Beyond the Pleasure Principle, 88
    childhood experiences, 7, 92
    Civilization and its Discontents, 67
    conscious and unconscious, 87
    death instinct, 69
    ego, 97
    Ego and the Id, The, 67
    ego-ideal, 132
    Inhibitions, Symptoms and Anxiety, 67, 88
    'Little Hans', 66, 88
    melancholic depression, 114–117
    mourning, 114
    neurosis, 14
    'On narcissism', 131
    phobia and panic, 77
    protective shield, 67, 88
    psychosexual theory, 17–20, 58
    regression, 58
    sexual trauma, 85–87
    Studies on Hysteria, 87
    superego, 117
    transference, 37
    unconscious, 50
    unobjectionable transference, 39–40

Gergely, G., 98
Glover, E., 48

Goncharov, I., 142
Green, A., 93, 137
Greenson, R. R., 38, 40
Grossman, V., 75
Grotstein, J. S., 36, 52
Gusnard, D. A., 99

Hartmann, H., 61
healing, 18, 21
Heimann, P., 48–49, 59–60
hysteria, 85–87 *see also* trauma

impasse
    analytic, 24, 39, 43, 44, 52, 90
    in dreams, 45–46
    transference psychosis as, 44–45
Impasse and Interpretation, 136
Inderbitzin, L. B., 60
intersubjective systems theory
        see psychoanalytic
        theories
Isaacs, S., 59–60

Jackson, J. H., 57–58
Jackson, S. W., 59
Jaffe, J., 13, 15, 98
Jaques, E., 101
Johnson, M. K., 99
Jones, E., 131
Joseph, B., 47, 49

Khan, M. R., 63, 71, 89
Klein, M., 20–22, 26, 106
    anxiety, 68–69
    clinical use of death instinct, 69
    countertransference, 49
    depressive position, 136
    good and bad object, 59
    narcissism, 135
    primary destruction, 119
    projective identification, 106
    regression, 59–60
    'On the sense of loneliness', 128
    transference, 38
Kohut, H., 24, 27, 133
    narcissism, 134–135, 137

regression, 62
self–object transference, 38
Kris, E., 60

Lachmann, F. M., 13, 15, 98, 138
LeDoux, J., 72, 78, 91
Levin, F. M., 91
Levy, S. T., 60
Little Hans, 66, 88
love, 19, 20, 60, 68, 69, 88, 101, 116–119,
        129, 131, 132, 133, 134
    –hate, 21, 59, 113
Lou, H. C., 99

Mancia, M., 28
melancholy, 58, 74, 88, 113, 117, 119
Meltzer, D., 70, 136
memory
    emotional, 28
    existential, 27
    explicit, 90, 91
    implicit, 90, 91
    self-, 99
    traumatic, 91
midlife crisis, 6, 101–102
Miller, F., 103
Modell, A. H., 12
Momigliano, L. N., 48
Money-Kyrle, R., 32, 50, 51
mourning, 69, 114–115, 117–118

nameless dread, 22, 70, 72, 73
narcissism, 62, 131
    benign, 133–135, 139
    considerations, 137–139
    destructive, 136
    features of, 132
    frustration, 134
    'good', 137
    infantile, 135
    libidinal, 136
    megalomania, 132
    negative, 135–137
    neuroses, 20
    organisation, 139
    primary, 133

thin- and thick-skinned, 136, 137
transference *see* self–object
    transference
traumas, 134
neuroscience, 3, 71, 78–79, 90–92, 98–99
    see also trauma
neurosis, 19–20, 66
Northoff, G., 100

object relations theory *see*
    psychoanalytic theories
Ogden, T. H., 52–53
Orange, D. M., 28
Ortu, F., 87, 91

panic *see also* anxiety; phobia and panic
    attack, 74, 75
    crisis therapy, 81–82
    disorder, 76
    and narcissistic defence, 80–81
    symptom, 82
paranoid–schizoid
    anxiety, 68
    position, 59
pathology, 23
    disorders, 102
patient, the, 150
phantasy, 20, 26
phobia and panic, 75, 83–84 *see also*
    panic
    cognitive therapy, 84
    fear pathways, 78–79
    neuroscientific contribution, 78–79
    psychoanalytic therapy, 84
    psychosomatic symptoms, 76–77
    thalamus–cortex–amygdale
        pathway, 78–79
    therapy issues, 81–83
physiological identity crises, 101–102
Pick, I. B., 50
post-traumatic stress disorder (PTSD),
    92 *see also* trauma
projection, 150–151
projective identification, 21, 22, 26,
    49–50, 70, 89, 106
protective shield, 67, 70, 71, 88

Psychic Retreats, 143
psychoanalysis, 1, 2–4, 7–8, 57
psychoanalytic theories, 17
    Bionian, 22
    intersubjective systems, 23–24
    object relations, 20–22
    psychosexual, 17–20, 58
psychosexual theory *see* psychoanalytic
    theories
PTSD *see* post-traumatic stress disorder
Putnam, F. W., 72

Racker, H., 51
reality principle, 118
reconstruction of past, 7, 11, 13–15
regression, 57–58, 63–64
    Balint and, 133
    and development, 60–61
    Kleinian, 59–60
    patient's depressive episode, 63
    types, 58
    Winnicott and, 61–63
Renik, O., 61
repression, 91, 150
Rosenfeld, H., 44, 103, 129, 135
    Impasse and Interpretation, 136
    narcissism, 136, 137

Sander, L. W., 138
Sandler, A.-M., 61, 90
Sandler, J., 61, 90
Schafer, R., 12
Segal, H., 77
self, 97, 128
    -harming, 103
    -memories, 99
    -object transference, 38
    -perception, 99
    -recognition, 99
    -reference effect, 100
    -reflection, 99
sexual abuse, 92–93, 94
sexuality, 19, 86
    infantile, 66
Spence, D. P., 12
Spillius, E. B., 49, 60

Spitz, R., 129
Steiner, J., 96, 143–144
Stern, A., 48
Stern, D. N., 138
Stolorow, R. D., 23, 27
Strachey, J., 48, 149
superego, 67, 74, 88, 112, 117, 132, 138, 151. *See also* anxiety; psychoanalytic therapy

Target, M., 98
transference, 21, 37 *see also* analytic relationship; countertransference
    Bion, 38
    Freud, 37–38
    illusory nature of, 38–39
    Klein, 38
    negative, 41
    neuroses, 20
    psychosis, 44–45
    unobjectionable, 39–40
transformational object, 41, 90
trauma, 85
    anxiety, 92
    basic fault, 89
    childhood neurosis, 88
    continued, 89
    cumulative, 89
    dissociation, 91, 92, 94
    early relational, 93–94
    emotional, 95
    environmental, 88–90
    explicit and implicit memory, 90, 91
    hysterical anxiety, 86
    memories, 91
    neuroscience, 90–92
    in primary relationship, 94–95
    psychic, 88
    trauma, 95
    repression, 91
    sexual abuse and sexualisation, 92–93
    sexual trauma and hysteria, 85–87
    and victimistic withdrawal, 96
Tronick, E., 13

unconscious, 4, 15, 18, 23–24, 31, 32, 36, 39, 40, 46, 69, 153 *see also* consciousness; dissociation
    Bion, 26–27
    consciousness and, 87
    and countertransference, 50–52, 53
    Freud, 25–26, 91
    Klein, 26
    melancholy, 114, 115
    relational, 27–29
    Sandlers, 90
    unrepressed, 28
unthought known, 27

Van der Hart, O., 87, 91
virtual reality, 142

Wahnstimmung, 106
Williams, P., 94
Winnicott, D. W., 27, 33, 70, 89
    facilitating environment, 130
    narcissism, 134, 135, 137
    and regression, 61–63
    self, 97, 107, 128
Wolf Man, 12, 66

Zimmer, C., 99